# What's On The Menu?!

Greetings Readers!

Welcome to yet another edition of Notes Magazine.

In honor of the recent anniversary of the bombing of the twin towers, we present a 1st hand account from New Yorker, Don Yorty, who was living and working in the city on that unforgettable day. Don gives us his take on the days following the bombings, without glamour or sensationalism, and captures the reality of the triumphant nature of the human spirit.

We also feature a spectacular new Spotlight Author in this edition, Lily Iona Mackenzie, a world-traveler who brings us along on a few of her journeys, both real and make believe. Other contributions this issue are as varied as the cultures in The Big Apple, as the climates on opposite continents—you will find thought provoking nonfiction examining the commonplace, the finite social standing of the word "Love", for instance, and on to explore outer space, in another philosophical essay examining the infinite view of nightscapes in relation to us little ole' earthlings. Our fiction offerings include some thrills, anti-romantic meanderings, office comedy, and even a little teen angst via text message.

As always, Notes brings a bit of everything to the table because Notes imitates life and life is a buffet that changes from hour to hour. Bon Appetite!

The Editors
Notes Magazine, The Grace Notes Foundation & Publishing

Visit www.GraceNotesBooks.com
For More Info on Notes Magazine,
GN Books, & The Grace Notes Foundation.
Check out our great subscription offers—
Get great reading enjoyment AND contribute
to a wonderful cause! GN is a Non-profit.

# Gifts that Give All Year...

**2013 Gift Subscriptions Now Available**
**The More You GIVE the More You SAVE!**

Grace Notes Books & Publishing is a division of The Grace Notes Foundation, a non-profit organization supporting the creative arts and writers. Gift subscriptions, offered savings up to 75% off, will offer up laughter, thought-provoking stories, entertainment, poetic arts, reviews on great books, films, television, and more, for the whole year—but also, as a non-profit, all funds are used to support our many supportive projects for literary artists as well as other creative! Support a worthy cause *and* make this holiday's gift the grace note of your season—and all year long!

# Or Check Out GN Reader's Book-a-Month Club!

**Reader's Club Membership Includes a Subscription to Notes**
**PLUS a Book-a-Month from Grace Notes Publishing,**
***Every Single Month Until 2015*****!**

In addition to Notes Magazine, GN Books publishes award-winning poetry, novels, memoir, and collections of short stories, personal essays, and more. All GN titles are stylized, including beautiful graphics, illustration, and cover art in combination with writings like none you'll find anywhere else. We look for and promote works that combine the artistic quality/integrity of 'literary' works with the entertainment value of mainstream books. So your friend or loved one will receive a year's worth of monthly laughter, thrills, tears (the good kind!), and mental stimulation.

These subscriptions are only available now, for the holiday's, and when you order your gift membership, GN will send the recipient (or you) a beautiful card wishing them a happy holiday (from you) and informing them of their new club membership details. Heck, you can even provide custom text to be printed in the card if you like, because we are just that cool!

Visit the foundation website to take advantage of this offer or to check out our other amazing seasonal gift ideas. Support our noble cause, and through us support the evolution of the literary arts-- *and* be the rockstar of gift-givers this year!

# www.GraceNotesBooks.com

# The Luck of Geography

Don Yorty

Tuesday morning was sunny and fresh, a lovely autumn day that made me happy to be alive as I walked to work at the Island School a few blocks away. I'd been given a new classroom that had a huge walk-in closet to hang up coats, but it was full of things set aside to fix, never to be touched again; useless old books, and boxes of dusty, broken, forgotten stuff. I was going to throw it all out, wanting my room to be an amiable place of order and calm, where my students would feel at peace and be able to learn.

My colleague, Nancy, interrupted my cleaning to tell me a plane had hit the World Trade Center. I said, and she agreed, "It must be a small plane with a couple of seats. The pilot had a heart attack and crashed, killing a few people and breaking a lot of glass," and that sadly was that, I thought, returning to my own mess. When Nancy stopped at my door again to tell me another plane hit the World Trade Center, I thought of terrorists, and walked to the principal's office. I could have gone out on the street to see the smoking towers, but I could imagine them well enough, and besides I was at work, and it seemed duty came first. When the principal urged us to go back to our rooms, I did and having no one to keep calm but myself, I started to clean again until I heard Nancy sobbing in the hall, with her face in her hands. Out of them she looked and said, "The buildings fell." It seemed like the floor gave way under me and I was falling too as I imagined all those people.

At the office, the staff gathering, Sharon, the secretary, was saying the buildings imploded. As a young woman, working for the Transit Authority, she assisted the architect who designed the World Trade Center and remembered the specs. "The buildings did not fall on any other buildings. They went straight down," she insisted, smiling. Sharon was a born again Christian and for her happily this was one step closer to the Apocalypse. Everyone else looked worried. A teacher was crying on the phone, another of the teachers had a daughter who worked at the World Trade Center and she was on the verge of hysteria, while another had turned her radio on and was upsetting the class. "Tell her to turn the damned radio off," Barbara, the principal, commanded, her mane

4

of gray hair flying. "Everybody get back to your classes. Let's keep things calm."

I had no class to get back to and when a mother appeared, desperate for her daughter, Sharon suggested, "Why don't you go get her." As soon as I returned and handed over the little girl, another mother appeared as desperate for her own child. The next hours blur, the Pentagon bombed, the plane going down in Pennsylvania, interspersed with mothers and fathers coming to get their children. One mother told me she worked at the World Trade Center, but was on a week's vacation. She really hugged her son. Every parent was concerned that terrorists were going to come and blow up the Lower East Side. What people love is what they fear to lose, no matter how inconsequential it may seem to the rest of the world. Fetching children made me feel like I was doing something and I was grateful for the job. Later, back in my classroom, I looked out the window down at the playground where even now some little girls were jumping rope. The wind was blowing through the lindens, the leaves upturned, and birds flying like nothing had happened or these human affairs mattered.

When I left school I noticed the smoke—the Towers were gone—billowing over the horizon going south toward Staten Island. There was hardly any traffic on Avenue D, which is a boisterous Hispanic street. People were walking around without making a sound as if God had turned the volume off. I had a beautiful view of the World Trade Center from my apartment windows. Back home I saw only smoke and knew that it was really gone. The night before I had gotten up to pee around four and looked at the Towers for a moment when I got back in bed. They were enchanting sentinels, ghostly, with red and white lights twinkling off of their great immensity, dominating and defining the nighttime sky.

I checked my answering machine. I heard my friend and neighbor Don Trammel screaming: "Don, get out of bed! Look out your window at the World Trade Center! Look at the World Trade Center!" Next was Neddi. She wanted me to call her at Gene and Brigid's. I did. Neddi was sure there was going to be another explosion, perhaps nuclear. To make matters worse, she couldn't call her mother in New Jersey; there was no long distance from Fifth Avenue where she was. From Ninth and C, I reached Neddi's mother, but couldn't get through to my sister Cathy in Pennsylvania, so I called Neddi's mom back to ask her to call my sister, but now I couldn't get through to New Jersey either. Then I dialed Pennsylvania and the phone was ringing. I told Cathy to tell everybody I was all right, but the phone might go dead at any moment. She was glad to hear my voice and I was glad to hear hers. Although many miles and a state away she seemed to be in the same state I was, shocked but involved. "All those firemen," she said.

I went up to the roof to take some photos of the smoke. Don Trammel was there. I told him by the time he called I'd already gone. He told me he was riding his bike to work when he heard a plane go overhead down Broadway so low that he looked up to read American Airlines on its side. Two blocks later at Washington Square, he saw the gash in the tower. Don thought he was looking at a movie set until he saw the flames. Ted, our neighbor, a journalist who had risked life and limb in Kosovo, was on the roof with his camera too. Ted had been up that morning and was annoyed that when the first tower fell the anarchists at See Squat on Avenue C had cheered on their rooftop like "their favorite team had just won." It was hard to believe Americans would find something to

5

celebrate in the deaths of fellow citizens whose only sin was getting up and going to work. These East Village anarchists, if they were with Osama bin Laden for a minute, he'd kick the beer bottles out of their hands and string them up stinking, faster than they hiss and spit at anyone who disagrees with them.

The billowing smoke was a crematorium that left us quiet on our rooftop. The roof on See Squat was empty; I figured once they'd realized everyone had seen them cheering, they went cowardly into hiding. I looked at all the people on the surrounding roofs and thought, "Let us live well and let evil know we'll not be cowed. But what we think is evil thinks we're evil. What's evil? That's the question at hand, the problem we have to solve."

Don, Ted and Neddi came to my apartment. None of us wanted to be alone. We sat together drinking vodka watching again and again on television the second plane hit the second tower. Neddi was determined to leave. She was sure there were going to be more attacks and was very anxious, as if every second was Russian roulette aimed at her head. I told her not to worry, that when you run from death, what you often do is run into it. But Neddi was adamant. We told her that everything was closed and jammed. How was she going to get out? But early next morning Neddi found a ferry going to Weehawken. With no planes in the sky and not much traffic on the Hudson it was beautiful and quiet. On the train from Newark she talked to a woman who had run out of the first building and in all the smoke got lost and wound up back where she had started, then she had to really run and luckily made it through all of the confusion. "She was our age," Neddi said calling from her mother's.

When the Towers collapsed, the pressure at impact heated to a thousand degrees, starting a fire beneath, that has to be hosed down constantly or it will burst into flames. Everybody's boots keep melting, having to be replaced. Wednesday morning the rest of the World Trade Center collapsed, sending smoke billowing north over NYU. When I left my apartment in search of a newspaper there was the smell of fire in the air, and burning plastic, which was unpleasant, but not overpowering. The streets were very quiet with hardly any but official traffic. Every now and then you heard a siren. Some people were walking around with dust masks or handkerchiefs over their faces. It was impossible to find a newspaper. Almost all newsstands are Muslim run and I smiled to let them know I wasn't angry with them. One fellow, his wife and I chatted. He didn't have any papers, but said the front page of the Post had the photo of two people jumping hand in hand from the Eighty-eighth floor. Hearing the sounds of a plane, we and everybody else on Fourteenth Street looked up warily to see two military jets streak overhead, feathering an otherwise untraveled sky. The south side of Fourteenth Street was blocked off to general traffic by the police and I had to show them my driver's license before they let me go home through the barricade.

Through the night the smell of smoke entered my dreams and woke me. Thursday morning the southern skyline was an oppressive fog that had erased City Hall and all the other buildings south of Canal. It was like nothing was there. I went to see a movie with my friend Gary. Sexy Beast was entertaining, made us forget, until we stepped from our air-conditioned reverie to stroll the smoky streets reminding us of death again. Like me, Gary wore no mask. We had to laugh when we saw two young gay guys, each wearing white dust masks, stop an older guy on his bike, excited to know where he'd bought the green plastic sci-fi-looking respirator he was wearing.

Only in the East Village does disaster turn into fashion.

Friday the blockade on Fourteenth Street was lifted. Now everyone can come and go as they please down to Houston. School would be open. It was raining, pouring, which made me glad. While I was still in bed drinking coffee, my cat Cachito ignored the cleansing weather and curled up by my thigh, with his paws over his eyes. I don't think he's noticed the change on the horizon, but then do we humans notice the anguish of animals, say the cries of an anthill stirred up and torn asunder by the sticks of little boys? I often feel, as a human, big and small at the same time, meaningless and yet the most important thing of all. Knowing one day I shall be dust and smoke, I got up and walked to work with a rolled up poster, a painting by Rousseau, The Snake Charmer, to hang up in the back of my classroom next to a map of the world.

There was some good news. The first grade teacher's daughter who worked at the World Trade Center had caught a cold and didn't go to work. Unfortunately a colleague had a friend who was a chef at Windows of the World, a young married man with a ten-month-old son. He hasn't come home. Later I took the bus—it was still raining—across Avenue D to C and then up Fourteenth Street to Union Square to get money from my bank where, out front, a little Asian lady was selling little American flags. At the south side of the Square before the dark statue of George Washington sitting stiffly on his horse, people were putting candles in a widening circle of photos and flowers and pieces of cardboard with written expressions of sympathy on them.

A few people moved among the candles extinguished by the rain,

dumped out the water and lit them again, the perfumed damp wax crackling and sputtering to flame as the ever changing crowd gathered around, stood and walked on. Here and there people played guitars and a circle of others holding hands prayed for peace in every country of the world, one guy calling out the names: "Let there be peace in Madagascar." *Let there be peace in Madagascar*. People had also constructed a wall of hope that curved along the lawn toward the east with hundreds of photos of people who haven't been found, most of them young, a father holding his newborn baby, a woman cutting her birthday cake, smiling at a party or the beach, some were old, a dignified man in a suit, lady executives and immigrants who cleaned the halls and bussed the tables at Windows of the World, in fact everyone in New York was on that wall.

I remembered 1990 in Guatemala when I stood in front of the post office in Santiago Atitlan where people from the countryside had hung up the photos of missing loved ones, hundreds of disappeared men and women, just after the Army had opened fire in the town killing and maiming dozens of civilians. The United States has supported a Guatemalan government that, since 1954, Eisenhower and the Cold War, has murdered a hundred thousand indigenous Guatemalans in the name of stamping out Communism. The wall in Union Square was like the wall in Guatemala, full of the faces of common people that no one will ever see again, done in by stern oppression. In that wall then and this wall now I could see no difference.

I stopped at Dick's Bar for a drink and talked to my friend Clio who heard the first plane go over as he was arranging flowers. He walked down Fifth Avenue and could see people hanging from the shattered towers, falling and jumping. He kept walking as the second plane hit. When the towers fell he stopped. David, who works at CBS, said the most difficult footage he ever edited was of his fellow New Yorkers jumping and letting go. He noticed that as the women fell, those wearing skirts held them down modestly to the very last second. It was this holding down of the dresses, David realized, that made us human. Curtis who has AIDS and lives at a hospice on Rivington Street was having a morning cigarette down in the garden when he heard a "Boom! Boom! Boom!" that he thought was thunder although the morning was sunny and brisk. When he went up to the roof, he saw what he thought had been an accident. It looked like a burning matchstick, just a little bit of flame shooting out. Loretta and Grant saw the first smoking tower on an elevated train coming into Manhattan. No one on the train reacted and for a moment they thought they were looking at special effects: "It takes awhile to wrap your brain around something like that." Curtis had a perfect view of the burning tower from the dining room. When the second plane hit, he

was watching it on television and turned to look out the window at the detonation of plane and building. At one with the explosion between heaven and earth, Curtis could not understand why he was alive while thousands of perfectly healthy people had just gone up in smoke. Danny had worked at the World Trade Center for a marketing firm, a psychiatrist who figures out the coming teenage trends. They'd done many fire drills before, evacuating the Towers, but nobody had ever told him what to do once he got outside, because he always went back in. Consequently hundreds of people were standing around, only moving further back until the rumbling started and everyone began to run trampling many, crushed and fallen, left behind. Danny never ran so fast in his life. Beyond thought, pure terror propelled him on to J & R Music World, where he stopped and looked around. Needing someone to talk to when the Towers fell, Curtis called Richard who lives on the Bowery and has a great view himself. Richard had seen the collapse and could hardly talk, while he and Curtis looked at the smoke, but then Richard said, as if out of breath, "Oh well, I never did like the architecture." We have to laugh. "They were too big," Curtis remarks: "Like two big dicks. Oh dynamic when you were standing right up next to them, but too much for such a small space. I hope the FBI isn't listening," Curtis whispers half in jest. I mention that on Fourteenth Street I saw American flag t-shirts for sale. Curtis bristles at the thought of wearing Old Glory. "I like flags in general, but let's face it, wearing the American flag is, is, is tacky! It's gaudy!" Curtis finally blurts out, making us chuckle, but then I'm somber: "You know, I was expecting a terrorist attack for a long time, but I always thought it would be germs in the subway or a suicide bomber in the Holland Tunnel or Radio City—"

Curtis cuts across me, saying, "--In the middle of a performance of Cats." Again we have to laugh.

On the way home from Dick's I noticed on every lamp post, wall and available space people had put up flyers with photos of their loved ones asking me to get in touch if I'd seen them, described down to the smallest detail, what clothes and jewelery they were wearing when they left home in the morning. It was so poignant, so stupid, so useless; every face I saw was dead. When I got home I saw Queen Elizabeth, Gerald Ford, and Jimmy Carter standing together at a funeral service on television, and something about the sad looks on their familiar faces made me start to cry, a quick eruption that startled Cachito who stretched up in my lap to look closely at my face, examining it strangely as I sobbed tears and snot. A man on television looking for his wife, held up her photo in case somebody had seen her. "Retaliation isn't the answer," he pleaded. "This has got to stop." A crowd in Jersey City attacked a car of Muslims, but luckily the police intervened. When a reporter asked the little Muslim boy how he felt about his attackers, he replied, "I want to kill them." The boy was born in Pakistan where they believe Mohammed gets you into heaven. I was born in Lebanon, Pennsylvania where Christ is coming back to raise the dead, as if the luck of geography predestines eternal salvation. On the island of Borneo in February, five hundred men, women and children were chopped apart, little girls sprawled headless in an Indonesian civil war hardly noticed or thought about, brought about, one could easily argue, by decades defunct old Cold War policy. What makes one death worthier than another? "The Mouth of Hell," Hillary Clinton called Ground Zero. I see open mangled space, pieces of the skeletal towers still standing, twisted burnt

wet, windows broken, knocked out but not down yet. Downtown's lit, smoke still rising, but the air is cool and fresh from the rain, washed it clean of human ash, the smell of rotting flesh. There is no moon or stars, the dome of heaven's endless, black but for two passing planes blinking transitory lights.

Saturday is bright. I ride my bike near but not next to the East River. Because of environmental laws enforced over the last twenty years, life is coming back into the waterways where not only fish, but barnacles and snails are living. After a century's absence, these creatures have returned and eaten, where they'd left off, into the wooden supports below the waterfront surrounding Manhattan. My favorite promenade is falling apart and now fenced off with no funding to fix it up. Until that long awaited day of reparations, I have to go like all the other bikers next to the FDR Drive, which is another kind of river that flows, comes and goes in its currents. Happy I ride, born from the struggling sperm into the yearning egg, conceived around the time Israel and China were born and shortly after Mahatma Gandhi was shot dead.

Oh you school children reading this one day on the moon, remember: "We the living think it's all about us, but it isn't." The pigeons come floating down at the very southern end of East River Park, not fenced off. I sit and see beyond the Brooklyn Bridge the State of Liberty, closed off to the public, surrounded by the Navy and the Coast Guard, raising her lamp in the fading sunset engulfed in the color of blood, the reddest of dusks. I asked my grandfather once if he believed in life after death. He was quiet as he thought about it. "There has to be more than this nightmare," he finally confided and we both had to smile a little bit.

◆━━━━━━━━━━━◆

# A Boy, a Hole, and the Ants

*E.S. Fay*

Men exactly like my father, stern and severe in combat boots, asparagus-green uniforms, often came by our house for tea. It was a special tea I suppose, unlike my mother's, since after ten o' clock, while they thought I was asleep in bed, I could hear their cups clinking, and they began to laughingly sing with pride and might and hoarse voices, voices coming out of the throats of mustached men, strong men who feared nothing.

Or so I thought they feared nothing, for my mother screamed one day at my father of how scared she was that things might turn bad soon and he had to quit the army. He had to take us to Uncle Odysseus in Australia, which at the time I thought must be some kind of a pretty house with a pool. That day my father said that he

was scared too, everyone was. That wasn't a reason to leave. Of course then, all I cared and thought about was the walk in the park next afternoon.

The day after my parents' confrontation marked, probably, my thirtieth time in the park.

It was there that I played the most, when Grandpa Grumpyface would take the liberty every other weekend to indulge me - the firstborn grandson – in walks, playground games and ice-cream, and by the thirtieth time all had changed.

The memory of first visiting the park is obscure, apart from a certain event. I'm not even sure there was a first time, but if there had been one it would be when this event occurred:

I, Alexander Stinson, could finally understand the calendar. I was seven, and it was only recently that I stopped presuming my age number was a measurement of height. Amongst the chunky trees providing about two acres of shade, I scraped my knee on the hard, caramel soil.

There was a fresh scent of eucalyptus, playfully intruded by a combination of cotton candy and salty popcorn coming from an aluminum trolley stand under a withered Coca Cola umbrella. I tried out the games, the slide, the trampoline, ran around to catch butterflies. Grandpa's orders had to be keenly followed. I, however, a young adventurer, ran when I shouldn't with shoe laces untied and fell down.

"Look what you've done," grandpa said, "Silly boy, you've killed the ants."

"Oh..." I exclaimed saddened, not knowing how to respond, but my frown was quickly erased, "But I haven't! There they are, running."

Grandpa's lips pleasantly stretched like bubble gum. He smiled partly because I had wised up, but more because I hadn't complained about the wound. But then I did say it hurt, my eyes narrowed, swelled.

"Come on buddy, no need for crying, the ants you killed would wish they were you. It serves them right for tripping you over."

I chuckled with a sniff. "But where are they grandpa? They're not here. I haven't killed them." I whisked the dirt off my knees and brushed my palm over the rough soil's surface looking for bodies.

"They must have gone up to heaven," grandpa said.

"Heaven?" I looked at him curiously.

"Yes, heaven - flew right up to the sky."

"Like Jesus?"

Grandpa scoffed, "Like Jesus."

"So I've helped them be with God! I've helped them! I've helped them!" I cheerfully stood up. Grandpa could not come up with a way to explain otherwise, nor did he have to, for he was saved when I took a step and my knee stung.

"Maybe we should go back home," grandpa said, "We have to ki- Take away the germs. With medicine. We are going to take away the germs with medicine and we are going to put them on a cotton wool. Like we did that time with your elbow."

That was my first time at the park, or at least the first time I think I remember. Of course then, I did get an ice-cream on the way back home.

I had learned later on about the holes the ants go in, their societies formed in the tiny cavities in the earth, the hard collective work they put into building their cities. Sometimes I would cover the hole to their colony, and until the next time I went back another one would have sprung up. I used a narrow stick to pave roads for these small friends I had made, let them follow it, and if they went astray I'd put them back on track. At some point I would decide to help them and crash them with the stick's end.

Despite grandpa's protests, we usually stayed at the park until sunset before we said goodbye to the trees and ants and the trampoline and the slide and the swing and went back home; a ritual grandpa came to perform with laziness and superficial interest.

On my thirtieth time there I tried to recall the way the park used to be, and I did so quite easily while I surveyed the altered grounds like a scientist observes a peculiar and dismal subject, scared to look but also awed to a point that prohibits aversion. The trees, all but three, lay on the ground like stems that had been stepped on; their roots ripped from the soil, dry and ragged, the trunks gnarled. I was holding grandpa's hand, close to the edge of an enormous hole.

"What's this hole, Pa? Did the ants get bigger? How did they make it? Did the ants pull down the trees?"

Before grandpa could shape his thoughts into a coherent answer, I continued with my inquisition.

"Why are these people on the floor? Why are my dad's friends lying in dirt? Are they helping ants? Like I did?" Thin smoke spread upwards from the terrifying hole and ashes danced carelessly in the soft breeze.

Grandpa spoke quietly, reluctantly, as if words stumbled in his throat. "No... I don't think there are any ants left."

"I think I know what it is grandpa. I think my dad's friends had too much tea. Tea can make you that way, act silly, sleep on the ground."

"Is that so Alexander?"

"Ma-hum!"

"Come on buddy, we have to keep moving, go to a special home for a while. We don't have much time."

"What's that sound grandpa?"

"Crickets son. Crickets shooting hoops,"

"But crickets can't lift the ball," I said as grandpa firmly led me away by the hand.

# Fellini Does Gatsby

Christina Bebeau

On the ride home Tim and his parents tossed around a lot of names and events I didn't know. There was a barbeque in the Hamptons (Worsthampton, as Tim refers to this particular town) for Sunday to which I was invited. I politely declined. They then went on to make fun of Tim's previous guest for not wanting to shower in the guest bathroom due to a lack of a curtain. Clearly, I would be self-conscious as fuck for rest of the weekend.

Tim had often mentioned his apartment on Park Ave, place in Jamaica (not Queens) and house on Long Island. Either I am comfortable enough with who I am and don't care about wealth, or maybe it's just that I am too self-centered and immediately forget everything everyone tells me about their lives to notice social class distinctions in my friends. I couldn't imagine anything intimidating about Tim, but upon arriving I found that his deck and pool house make up what could be the perimeter of my father's house. And my father, a doctor at a major pharmaceutical company whose technical title includes the words "Global Expert," does not have a small house. But million dollar Toll Brothers McMansions are a dime a dozen in New Jersey while New York and L.A. wealth are a completely different ball game.

When we pulled into the garage, I noticed a yellow Ferrari as well as some other cars I had never seen. They mentioned "the Rolls" and some fancy Italian car I am not rich enough to recognize. The Lexus SUV we had been driving was obviously their cheapest car. These are cosmopolitan Northern Italians, not my crazy family from Bari in the South, the town about which sheep fucking jokes originated. Meanwhile, I am from New Jersey, have no class, steal bar glasses from restaurants, and have an Aunt Dina and an Uncle Vito. My mother was an immigrant and came through Ellis Island when she was four. On my father's side, my grandfather was in the Marines before becoming a railroad conductor. That's pretty fucking American. Both sides were raised in New York City, my mother's Bensonhurst upbringing seeming like *An American Tail* while my father in Jackson Heights seemed to grow up in an episode of *Hey Arnold!* I'm generally proud of the whole embodiment of the American Dream thing.

There was Tim's sister Caroline, a blondish prettier Melissa Joan Hart type (without the negative lameness connotation of Melissa Joan Hart), and her boyfriend Andrew, an almost fratty med-school student. I met Marcus, who looks like a young Michael Douglas, a friend of the family who was wearing blue shorts and a polo with a navy sweater hanging on his shoulders. Up to this point I thought the shoulder sweater was just a Ralph Lauren catalog myth and not something that people actually did. I was also introduced to Tim's grandparents who only spoke Italian. Lastly there were Tim's parents, Jonas and Isabella. Jonas is great but when I am older I want to be like Isabella. It's not just the way she reminds me of Edie Monsoon from *Ab Fab,* it's the way she tells stories and scrunches up her face when she smiles and laughs. She is a genuinely

12

happy adult. I don't know how many of those I've ever actually met.

My feet were disgusting from walking around the city all day in flip flops and I felt like everyone was staring at them. Or were they staring at my chipped toe nail polish? I'd never given much thought to toe nail polish before now. Did I look sweaty from being on the subway and running errands all day? Or were my boobs falling out of my dress- and could they tell I had done alterations on it myself? Did they think it was weird that I was wearing a tank top under the dress to make it slightly more conservative? Or the opposite, did they think my boobs were everywhere despite my tank top's attempts to cover them?

As if I wasn't uncomfortable enough, they remembered that I hadn't eaten and Tim took me around to two different refrigerators (I don't know why this was so intimidating, we have two fridges, too) in hopes of securing some snacks, all the while talking about how his mother could make me something. I hate being waited on- it's part of why I have trouble being a guest. I am much more comfortable putting away my own dishes and getting my own food because I don't want to feel like I am imposing. My mother always made it feel like having anyone do anything for you was wrong. When she would offer to get things for me or clean up from dinner, I would always be guilt tripped about it later. I think she just liked cleaning and getting people things so that she could hold it over their heads because if she hadn't, she would probably have no other contribution to humanity to brag about. But that weekend I was one of many guests and Tim assured me that his mother loved entertaining. So when Isabella asked me if I liked smoked salmon, I had to say yes despite my natural inclination to refuse everything in order to not impose, which would go against my other natural inclination to eat smoked salmon whenever possible. Also,

they are Jewish and it struck me as something of an amusing stereotype that they just happened to have lox and cream cheese just sitting around the house.

Isabella looked in the fridge and asked Tim about some Rolling Rock and Mike's Hard Cherry Lemonade inside. He said his friends brought them. She then asked him in her refined Northern Italian accent "why did they bring such douchey drinks?" In my youth my mother was always obsessed with manners, adhering to a strict code of what is ladylike and what was taboo at the dinner table. She would never in a million years refer to anything as "douchey," but here Isabella, the most sophisticated woman I have ever met, was using it to categorize her son's friend's choice of alcohol. This was the moment when I first fell in love with Tim's family. Like being in Fellini movie, I created an impression of what I thought was the established universe only to have it turned on its head moments later with every new piece of information added. While *Amarcord* is a fitting picture of my mother's family, these people are obviously of *La Dolce Vita*. The outsider feeling in a Long Island setting added to wealth and the host's proclivity to throwing parties christened this in my mind as Fellini's adaptation of *The Great Gatsby*.

Upstairs, Tim and his mother made the guest bed for me. I sat on the couch opposite the bed but moved because I didn't want my head to hit the original cubist painting hanging above it. I tried not to assume that it was an original Picasso but it probably was. Who would hang an original Picasso in a guest room? It was one of many interesting accoutrements around the house, including the *Un Americana A Parigi* poster hanging above the landing (the house is three stories, a perfect companion to my irrational fear of stairs), the large poster of Ronald Reagan's face with the word "ACTOR" in bright blue letters in the theatre, pictures I mentioned I liked only to be told "those are Warhols", plus books in the guestroom. On one nightstand sat *Slow Food Nation* and Michael Moore's *Stupid White Men* while the opposite nightstand had a copy of *Calvin and Hobbes Homicidal Psycho Jungle Cat*.

I had my period and for some stupid reason didn't bring any extra pads for the night, only tampons for the day which I never wear to sleep due to a penchant for sleeping ten hours each night and an irrational fear of Toxic Shock Syndrome. I was uneasy about interrupting the merriment from downstairs to ask for one and figured that the one I was wearing would get me through the night just fine. I worried that I would get blood on their pristine off white sheets until this worry was overtaken by the worry that the toilet would blow up. For shits and giggles I had turned on the Japanese heated toilet seat but could not figure out how to turn it off, another thing I did not want to ask anyone.

The following morning I woke up to a single red dot on the sheets. What do I do? They'll see it when they strip the sheets or even turn down the bedspread. Maybe since they have a cleaning lady she will deal with the laundry and I have nothing to worry about. But the only thing to do is to strip the sheets as insurance that I will not be lured to stay another night and go to a Gatsby party in the Hamptons. I will instead return to my friend's BBQ in Brooklyn and awkwardly hold a beer but not drink any of it because I don't like beer but it's Park Slope and they won't serve anything else and I won't want to seem rude or ungrateful.

I stripped the sheets. I can say that I was uncomfortable that his mom was doing everything and I wanted to help out, which was very true. While I was putting this plan into action, however, I noticed a smaller blood stain on the mattress protector (originating at the

stain on the sheets but mostly just a stain on this vacation). I considered putting the sheets on the stain to cover it but then it would only be more obvious that I was trying to cover it so I instead put them at the foot of the bed and hoped that someone would notice the sheets before the stain.

And I know that I sound like a bad female comedian by talking about this therefore furthering the untrue notion that the only things women ever talk about are their periods and how big or small their boyfriends dicks are, but is it completely paranoid to obsess over a bloodstain on someone else's sheets resulting from a completely normal yet mildly taboo bodily function? But that it is so normal and controllable is exactly what makes this such a difficult situation. If it's so normal, why couldn't I prevent the stain on the bed in the first place? I took all normal measures to avoid such a situation. But if I did, then why is there a stain on the sheets? Because I didn't want to tell a person I just met about my period? Because Tim's mom might be past menopause anyway and might not have any pads in which case I would have told her for nothing, therefore becoming one of those girls who tells you about her period for no reason. Because my mother has seared on my brain the importance of not imposing on other people? Because I didn't want to disturb Caroline in her room with her boyfriend to ask about pads and risk possibly walking in on two people I just met doing it in their own house? Because I didn't want to ask for pads for fear of being seen as irresponsible about packing for a trip? For being seen as weird for wearing pads instead of tampons to sleep to avoid TSS because, as a result of being raised in a pharmaceutical family, I have no desire to put myself in danger of any illness that would then lead to me being put on any kind of drugs?

14

Next order of business: showering. Well, I am only staying for today and since I showered before I left last night I technically don't really need to shower until tonight and won't be dirty if I don't shower. And I'll probably want to shower later since we'll probably go to the beach and I'll be all greasy from sunscreen and gross from the water. But they don't know when I showered last and my feet are disgusting and I do have my period and I don't want them to think I am dirty. There are a thousand towels and a personal bathroom in this guestroom so there is no worry of having to be seen by anyone in a towel and really no downside to showering.

Except for this shower. There are no curtains in this bathroom. They made fun of the last guest for complaining about this-- I thought they were talking about shower curtains, not window curtains, so voicing any opposition to a lack of a curtain or using this as an excuse for not showering was absolutely out of the question.

I stripped uncomfortably in front of the window and felt a little better when I stepped inside the transparent glass shower door, even though it was transparent. I turned it on and a few drops of water dropped from the end of the shower. There was clearly something wrong with the water pressure. I tried wetting my hair, thinking this shower would be annoying but not intolerable, but there really wasn't enough water. I turned on the faucet and the water poured in the tub full force. I pulled the knob to turn on the shower. Again, almost no water. I ran the tub, tried to clean myself, shifted into uncomfortable position after uncomfortable position under the faucet, got frustrated, turned on the shower again, realized that there wasn't enough water coming out to rinse my hair, ran the tub, flipped my hair upside down and rinsed it under the full force of the water, got scared

that my hair would get stuck in the drain, turned on the shower, got frustrated with the lack of water, turned on the tub again, rinsed my hair, thought that my hair would probably look ridiculous from being rinsed this way and worried that I wouldn't be able to fix this because I didn't have any mousse with me and didn't want to ask for any, rinse and repeat. I did this a few more times, hoping to fix the shower before realizing that the family was probably awake and could hear what the symphony of a moronic guest unsure of how to use a system of running water found in every bathroom in America. And all of Long Island was watching me fail at showering since there were no curtains.

I got dressed and instantly felt self-conscious for bringing a shoddy tank top (with a rip in the armpit!) and some mass-produced plaid shorts, even though this was appropriate attire for summer fun. This was the first time I encountered their cat Des (sort for Desdemona, a great name for a cat). She is an old longhaired cat with a flat face. Like the rest of the family, I felt mildly intimidated by her, not because I think the cat is better than me, but because one of her eyes is squinty as if she is always raising a sarcastic eyebrow in my direction. "Are you really going to wear that, you uncultured New Jersey trash?" The cat seemed to say. The entire household is judging me. The cleaning woman gave me something to eat and I said gracias, out of habit. She corrected me in front of Isabella, thinking I was trying to speak Italian but was not smart enough to differentiate between the two languages.

Only the Roomba was awake save for Marcus, sitting on the deck with his laptop. He said he had eaten already so I went into the kitchen and fixed another lox and cream cheese sandwich. Isabella entered the kitchen and I felt instantly strange at helping myself to the very food I had been offered last night. Mostly it was

15

just that I realized that unlike my family, these people were actually a real family and probably ate as one. Should I have waited for everyone to wake up to see if they would prepare and eat breakfast together? But then if I had waited for them to wake, would that only pressure them into making breakfast for me (because why else then would I be waiting?) when I could have easily made it myself? I tried to reassure myself that Marcus probably knew that they didn't eat breakfast together or else he wouldn't have gotten anything to eat before the family woke up. Or it was because he was practically family and had no problem with helping himself to breakfast unlike some random girl they had just met. Isabella didn't seem to care and turned on the World Cup, mentioning rooting for Germany. Strange that Jews would want Germany to succeed at anything.

The next time I saw the guestroom, the mattress protector was also stripped from the bed. Someone saw the sheets and took them and also decided to wash the mattress protector. Did they strip the mattress protector because of the stain or because they always wash the mattress protector? Are you supposed to wash the mattress protector? Do they think I am dirty because I didn't also strip the mattress protector, especially when it WAS COVERED IN MY BLOOD? Did they see the stain on the mattress protector, regardless of whether I was supposed to also strip the mattress protector, and as a result of that, decide to wash the mattress protector and also check the sheets for further stains? I really wish someone would just mention the damn thing so I could say I didn't notice it and I'm sorry. At least it would be out in the open and I could stop running my brain in circles over blood stains like a neurotic Lady MacBeth, paranoid about this family laughing at me when I leave, telling the story of the girl who rudely got blood on their sheets and tried to cover it up by

stripping the sheets and not mentioning it in hopes that nobody would notice. That's funnier than the weird friend who wouldn't shower because there weren't curtains and left his Rolling Rock in the fridge with our Prosecco. Boy Tim, you sure do know how to pick friends.

Tim's mother had asked him if the stripped sheets meant I was leaving and I said yes.

I tried to forget about the sheets and actually had a good time until I was struck like a ton of bricks with the unfortunate aroma of bell peppers wafting out the window. I have always been afraid of my reaction to eating a food I do not like while at dinner with unfamiliar company- I do not want to be rude and worry that someone would always be watching me eat to see if I like something or not. This rarely happens, however, because there are very few things I do not like. I do not drink coffee, but coffee is usually offered and rarely forced. But bell peppers and I have been sworn enemies my whole life. I hate them so much that I even devote a paragraph to voicing this on my OKCupid profile ("Sometimes I pretend I am allergic to red peppers so there is no chance that someone will forget to omit them from my foodstuffs, sparing me a detailed tirade such as this of my lifelong loathing for them, and avoiding the unfortunate instance where I will undoubtedly act like an autistic child should red peppers be on or anywhere near my food.") My family knows I don't like them so they either don't cook them or don't get offended when I don't eat them. Even my evil stepmother from my youth would make Clams Casino sans the peppers when she prepared it on Friday nights. I am not a good enough actress to pretend I like them, either.

People were starting to sit down to dinner and unaware of where to sit, I took a seat next to Marcus, thinking that Tim would sit on my other side. Instead, Tim's grandfather sat next to me. Will I be awkward and only speak to

Marcus the entire dinner or will Tim shout across the table obnoxiously to try to engage me in conversation and then the two of us will seem rude? Or will Marcus and Tim both completely ignore me, leaving me to sit quietly in a sea of Italian voices?

First course: Satan's appetizer, bell peppers. I felt my mother ready to flog me with a book of manners. These peppers were covered in melted cheese. As an American, I enjoy most things more when prepared with unnecessary amounts of cheese. I cut one piece of pepper into a few smaller bits, trying to decide whether to ration my cheese to fit over each piece when there clearly was not enough cheese to manage, or whether I should instead put the majority of the cheese on a few bits to make them almost edible and then leave the other few bits on my plate. Certainly I would not be looked down upon for not finishing a few small bits of pepper. Meanwhile in reality, I was being harassed in Italian by Tim's grandfather about why I only took one slice of pepper.

I ate the cheese. I ate a bit of pepper and tried to cover up the inevitable whiskey face to follow by chasing it quickly with a bit of Pellegrino, only to notice that my glass for some reason smelled of dog. Luckily, soon after this, his grandfather poured me some white wine, which made an excellent chaser. I wish I had more of it to chase the wine we drank with the main course, which was not but tasted like Marsala.

His grandfather tried to teach me a bit of Italian. He was surprised I already knew the word from my mother and asked where she was from. He drew a map of Italy with his hands and pointed to the North and the South and asked me to show where she was from. I cringed, pointing to a point near the heel of the boot. There was palpable judgment and disappointment in his face. He turned to

Isabella and asked her, in Italian, why if my mother spoke Italian, then why didn't I know Italian? She shrugged and agreed it was strange. Even with my limited abilities in the language, I understood this and was mortified.

On the drive to the train station, Tim and his father invited me to come back after the Hamptons and Brooklyn barbeques. I agreed before I was hit with the familiar barrage of questions from myself: If I go back will they just put the same sheets I used back on the bed since there is no use in washing them if I will be there again? Or will a guest arrive and stay in that room and they will change the sheets? Or, when a guest arrives, will they deliberately put them in a different room to keep me in the same room?

I went to the party in Brooklyn and tried my best to look like I was actually drinking my PBR and not just glaring at the abundance of irony. I did little else at home other than sleep, shower, attend the barbeque and paint my toenails. Tim's family would be the type to actually notice chipped toenail polish if that hadn't been entirely in my imagination. I heard my mother's voice in my head fretting over her chipped nail polish, remembering how stupid a thing I always thought it was. I regretted that today was the day I finally made the transformation into my unfortunate mother.

When I arrived, Jonas and Isabella wanted to do karaoke and got very excited about the idea of playing Rock Band. I was in a different guest room because someone else was in the room where I had been staying. The sheets on this new bed were blue, not off white, had no blood stains, but did have some bleach spots. Did they get the blood stains out of the sheets on the other bed? I did not want to venture into a stranger's room to find out. Did they notice the blood on the other sheets? Did the cleaning woman notice the blood stain on the sheets before putting them in the wash? If not, did they come out in the wash and if they didn't, did she notice them then? Does she always bleach the sheets, resulting in the bleach stains on the blue sheets, or were these bleached for a particular reason? Would the bleach even get out the blood stain out? In any case, if the cleaning woman noticed the blood stain, would she mention it to Isabella?

Before going to sleep, I noticed that there was not only no curtain on the window in this bathroom but also no shower curtain. In fact, no shower, just a bath. At least the other shower had a translucent glass door. Perhaps tomorrow the other half of Long Island that did not watch me yesterday will watch me do my ever-popular guest bathroom bathing routine.

I woke up early. Please let there not be a blood stain on the bed. If there had been, the attempt to bathe myself bit might have turned into an attempt to drown myself. If I strip these sheets as well, it will make it look like I was just trying to be a good guest and was not at all trying to hide anything the first time around.

So I got up, stripped the sheets, went to the bathroom to shower. No shampoo. I went downstairs to ask Tim for some but he was still asleep. The person in the guest bedroom opposite Tim's was awake and had made the bed or else the cleaning woman had. Do they think I am crazy for stripping the sheets from the bed? Isn't that a normal thing to do when you are a guest in someone's house? I wandered in, hoping to find shampoo, but then felt like it would be weird to be caught snooping around rather than just asking someone for it. I don't really need to shower anyway. By now you must think I am a very dirty person having twice tried to avoid showering but this weekend it just seemed as if the universe did not want me to be clean. Regardless of wanting to shower here or not, I of course still have to look like I showered. I went back upstairs sans shampoo and turned

on the tub. I wet my hair with the sink water. I saw a t-shirted individual outside and realized what I was facing was the service entrance to the house and the woman must be the cleaning woman. Did she see me? She walked away and I only saw her back. I have wet hair so I at least look like I showered. If asked, I'd say I had shampoo in my backpack. Downstairs, both Tim and his mother at separate times complimented my newly blue toenails. I rolled my eyes at my mother from a hundred miles away, hating her for being right.

I was excited to hear that we were going tubing and waterskiing, two of my favorite summer activities. But first we had to partake in one of my favorite anytime activities, eating. So after another healthy dose of lox and cream cheese on toast, the family by now thinking I had an unhealthy obsession with salmon (not entirely untrue), we were off and it was minimally humiliating.

Isabella prepared a lovely lunch. She was particularly excited about a large container of marinated artichokes because it "was a steal at Costco for $6."

As Tim drove me to the train station, I told him I was writing about the trip.

"Can I read it?"

Never. Never ever in a million years.

"I'll probably never get around to writing it anyway."

On the subway back to my world, a baby cried. I felt more at home on that train than I had all of that weekend, sitting in the quintessential representation of working class misery. As much as I seem to look down as on the idle rich for relaxing and having a good time partying, I really can't blame them. Would I even remember this vacation if it hadn't been a complete mindfuck of a desire for social acceptance? The crying baby said it all: *La Dolce Vita* is over and it's time to go back to *Annie Hall.* That's where you belong.

# Fogs and Beer

*Zdravka Evtimova*

The lakes in Josaphat Park in Brussels were heavy with pale, sickly water lilies. The benches looked forlorn and moldy. Thick crowds of ravens hung above the trash cans, glum birds, bigger than the clouds. It rained constantly, day and night.

Josaphat was the centre of the Arab neighborhood in Brussels. Here the women walked slowly, majestically. Heavy women wrapped up in brown veils, followed by clusters of children, big and small. The braver boys fed the ravens, the girls led their mothers by the hand diligently, dutifully, talking to each other in beautiful, soft voices. I watched them every day as I practiced speaking French in Chez Albert, the cheapest pub in the park.

Albert, the owner of the place, asked me to make Bulgarian salads for his customers, all of them pensioners who lived in the imposing building, La Maison Communale, across the street, which he also owned. The old gentlemen believed it rained specially for them. Each would tell me maybe this was the last rain they would ever see, and thanked me for it, as if it was me who had given them the sky and the clouds.

"*Ma cherie*, let's work on *le futur proche*, or if you prefer we can choose another tense," one of them, Monsieur Duchemin, would beseech me every afternoon. He told me that a man had died on every step of the narrow staircase of La Maison Communale, from the first floor to the last. "Monsieur Fishgrund, for example, may meet his maker soon, *ma cherie*," Duchemin told me one day. "Albert should make him pay his rent in advance. One never knows with us, we old fellows."

I lived in Maison Communale too, but I didn't actually pay Albert rent. He "visited" me one or more nights a week, always *très gentil*, very kind. On those evenings he brought wine, cooked our dinner, and lit candles. Of course it always rained, but if suddenly the clouds sank to the bottom of the sky and the raindrops died on the roofs, Albert would say, "Let's go for a walk in Josaphat, *ma cherie*."

There were times when I hated the park. You see, I worked for a retired infantry-major, Jacques, who, in his residence at La Maison Communale, wrote novels for five hours every day. In the evenings I edited his prose, feeling his words and his eyes on my skin, his cat, all the time, purring in his lap. The retired major was Albert's best friend.

I hated going for walks with them in Josaphat, so often the two friends jogged side by side in the drizzle, while I stayed back and made salads for the pensioners, listening to them debate whether Monsieur Duchemin would piss in his pants before dinner, and who would later accompany me to my apartment, Albert, or the major—the old guys called the

## Winterscape: Snow Vs. Crow

Like billions of dark butterflies
Beating their wings
Against dreams, or myriads of
Spirited coal spread from the sky
Of another world, a heavy black snow
Falls, falling, fallen down
Towards the horizon of my mind
Where a little white crow
Is trying hard to fly
From bough to bough

*Changming Yuan*

major *Jacques le Fou*, Crazy Jacques.

Often, after jogging was over, Albert and the major would toss a coin to decide just who was to "walk me home" that night, a term I considered absurd, since the three of us lived in the same building. The tenants in this La Maison Communale, the pensioners, went to bed at 8 pm, dreaming about rain. From time to time Crazy Jacques appeared on TV and spoke cleverly and at length on his books and his understanding of the world. On nights when he won the toss, he cooked, say, *filet mignon brusselois* with white wine for me, but very often in the middle of the *filet mignon brusselois* he would blurt out, "We should hurry up," which meant that the evening would follow the scenario I knew all too well.

If Albert won the toss, he would arrive at 9 pm sharp, whereas Crazy Jacques was often "ready" even before 8:30. Jacques's love was like a dry and voluminous TV show, like the ones in which he took part. He never told me I was pretty, never said I was pleasant company, and I wondered why he kept on tossing the coin in that cold park for the late-evening time with me.

Probably Crazy Jacques really only showed up in my apartment in order to describe the episode later in one of his experimental novels—he had already written three of them in which I was the protagonist, a woman who arrived in the clean, generous city of Brussels from Eastern Europe to look for truth and to learn to speak French. In all three novels I, though not quite cleverly, was Monsieur Jacques's beloved, whom he took from under his best friend's—that would be, but with a fictional name, Albert's—nose. Jacques' novels were highly praised if unreadable, and it constantly rained in them; not a single page with sunny weather.

Crazy Jacques liked to ask me why didn't I marry Monsieur Duchemin. "The old grouch admires your salads, *ma cherie*. All in Maison Communale know that. He'll die soon, and you'd inherit his collection of Belgian banknotes, which is quite substantial. He has a good car and, as far as I know, he owns a *magnifique* villa in the town of Ghent, which he rents out."

"I can't marry him because either you or Albert—after tossing a coin—will show up five minutes into the honeymoon," I said.

Chez Albert was the strangest pub in the neighborhood. Albert sold only fruit beer. There was cherry beer, which the pensioners nicknamed "Sweet July death", mountain berry beer, and a special brand of diet carrot beer. Albert came by to give me a test in French immediately after his best friend, the retired Major le Fou, took his dry love back to his splendid always-parked car, the one he bought at an advantageous price from a dying pensioner. After love was over, Monsieur Jacques le Fou often left his old electrical appliances for me as tokens of his appreciation.

"I almost never touched them, *ma cherie*." Jacques said. "An iron, but what an iron! It's produced by the renowned French company Braun! There is a washing machine for you! And that bicycle is a Shimano!' Two vacant apartments in our building were stuffed with objects Crazy Jacques had given me as presents. He liked it when his love blazed a tangible trail in its wake. "Is Albert better than me?" Jacques asked me. "Did he recite to you some of his new poems?"

Yes, he is "better" than you, I silently admitted to myself.

Albert wrote his poems in a way that made me think of the pensioners' very last rain, and of the sweetish fruit beer they drank in Chez

Albert. Albert recently penned that on July 15th it would stop raining, because in July he loved me the way the sky loved its clouds, quietly and sadly. "Tomorrow the rain will be for you, *ma cherie*," he wrote. Albert's love was peaceful, like beer made of forest berries, timid and aromatic, doing no harm, its sparkling depths as infinite as my dreams about Bulgarian summers. His love made me imagine I sat in a village pub with an old drunkard who had a row of empty glasses on the table in front of him. Though I just knew it rained outside that pub too, and its parking lot was perpetually empty.

Albert never asked me about Crazy Jacques' new novel, and never said his best friend the major was crazy. He called him "my poor old friend: My poor old friend Jacques wrote again in a novel that he stole you from me."

In summer when the Brussels afternoons, tired of their battle against the rain, would call it a day and go to to sleep under the roof of some deserted bus stop, Albert would close the pub until the evening. Then the three of us, Crazy Jacques, radiant after his umpteenth TV appearance, Albert and I would go out together to get drunk on vodka. We drank in the garden behind Crazy Jacques's so-called "holiday villa". I sat between them, feeling their arms about my shoulders. We drank and hugged, we held each other, our shoulders pressing tightly; we took slow quiet walks along Avenue des Mimosas. I strode in the middle, one man to either side of me, and it rained all over the place. Jacques had bought an enormous piece of oilcloth. We hid under it, wrapping it tightly around us and ambled on until Avenue des Mimosas melted under the wet raincoat of the sky. We felt the wind in our bones, and at Meiser Square the two men again prepared to toss a coin for me.

I wondered who was to see me off to sleep that night. Would love be a pine forest and a country pub, or would it be a glamorous and silly TV show? Sometimes I didn't want them to toss that coin, I took it from them and threw it into the fountain, then we'd stand under the streetlamp until one of them came up with another coin.

"What if you and I ran away to the Netherlands," Jacques said, "and left Albert in the lurch? What do you say to that?" Yes, Jacques le Fou asked me this one day, but I already knew such could never happen. Albert was his best friend. Yet there were reasons I was Jacques le Fou's best friend too.

But I knew I couldn't go on living like that. Anyway, I was sure all would end on July 15th when, Albert promised me, there would be sun in the sky—but didn't the oilcloth feel wonderfully cozy when the three of us huddled together under it, the rainy evenings beautiful like kisses all along the way to Pierard Avenue? Walking, hugging, I between the two men, and Meiser Square heavy with the moon, it folding around our shoulders.

"You are very pretty," Albert said to me, but Jacques snorted, "Don't believe his lies."

Then Albert said, "Stay with me—if it doesn't rain on July 15th, I marry you, and Jacques can marry his French publisher. Let us leave the rain to toss the coin for us!"

Every evening, as I watched the quiet Arab women taking walks in Josaphat Park, wrapped in their brown silence and black clothes, flocks of children babbling in their wake, I wished I were a raven trying to perch on their hands.

When the 15th of July came it rained so badly that the streets turned to streams. Monsieur Duchemin was still alive and phoned asking me to become his wife.

Albert and Jacques waited in Chez Albert, and although the 15th was a Saturday night

# Epilogues: A Parallel Poem

Just as both God and Devil are man's incarnation, so are Heaven and Hell both man's construction.

I

From the front yard of a melodious morning
From the busy road of a sweet Saturday
From the moist corner of a heavy march
From the back lane of pale winter
We have come, here and now, all gathering
In big crowds gathering in big crowds
Gathering in ever-bigger crowds gathering
For the boat to cross the wide wild waters
Before the fairy ferry is fated to fall
Under our feet too heavy with earthy mud

II

You may well hate Charon
But you cannot help feeling envious:
That business of carrying the diseased
Across the River Styx is ever so prosperous
The only monopoly in the entire universe
That has a market share
Larger than the market itself
Daydreaming, on this side
Of the river, how you might wish
To be an entrepreneur like him
A success American dreamer

III

Flying between sea and sky
Between day and night
Amid heavenly or oceanic blue
I lost all my references
To any timed space
Or a localized time
Except the non-stop snorting
Of a stranger neighbor

Then, beyond the snorts rising here
And more looming there
I see tigers, lions, leopards
And other kinds of hunger-throated predators
Darting out of every passenger's heart
Running amuck around us
As if released from a huge cage
As if in a dreamland

*Changming Yuan*

Albert had closed the pub early and they were drinking vodka inside when I arrived.

"It's raining," Crazy Jacques said, smiling.

It was a long way to Meiser Square where we went every time to toss the coin.

"What will you do with Monsieur Duchemin?" Albert asked me, very seriously—but even a glancing contemplation of what my answer might be made me shy away from all thoughts of the past and the future.

Then the three of us—I, as always, between them, Jacques on my right, Albert to the side of the privet hedge—trudged through the clouds and rain to Meiser Square. Our clothes became sodden within seconds.

"There's no use tossing a coin," Albert said suddenly. "Because it feels to me as if the sun is shining. In fact, it's the brightest sun Brussels has had for two centuries now!" The rain continued to pour down.

First I thought of that distant-village pub—and Albert—but then suddenly I thought more deeply of Crazy Jacques: I was his novels' eternal protagonist, after all, so I, not Albert, was actually his best friend.

There was a 50% chance—

"We'd better toss a coin," I said.

◆———————————————◆

Notes Magazine's
Spotlight
Author
Lily MacKenzie

Lily Iona MacKenzie has crossed many borders in her life, moving from Calgary, Canada, to the San Francisco Bay area as a young woman. An avid traveler, she has journeyed all over the world, just recently completing a trip to Scandinavia, St. Petersburg and Moscow.

She also travels every night to exotic places and has kept a dream journal for many years. These experiences inseminate her writing, which ranges from poetry, short and long fiction (she's written four novels), non-fiction (she has a collection of essays), to children's stories. For two years, she co-created a radio program called "Aunt Sally's Story Shoppe" in Marin County. She and her partner adapted traditional fairy tales and myths, as well as their own stories, for an audience of children and adults.

A high school dropout and a mother at 17, Lily was once a groupie, hanging out with Ronnie Hawkins and the Hawks. Levon Holmes and Robbie Robertson were then part of the group before they created The Band with Bob Dylan.

Over the years, she has supported herself as a stock girl in the Hudson's Bay Company, as a long distance operator for the former Alberta Government Telephones, and as a secretary (Bechtel Corp sponsored her into the States). She also worked as a cocktail waitress at the Fairmont Hotel in San Francisco, briefly broke into the male-dominated world of the docks as a longshorewoman (and almost got her legs broken), founded and managed a homeless shelter in Marin County, and eventually earned two Master's degrees (one in English with an emphasis on Creative writing and one in the Humanities). She now teaches writing part-time at the University of San Francisco and is vice-president of the part-time faculty association, a position that allows her to fight for social justice.

All of the arts inspire her, and she dabbles in painting and assemblage when she isn't writing, messing around in her garden, working out at the gym, or spending time with her husband.

# A Doll's House Redux

*Lily Iona Mackenzie*

I couldn't have brought home Grandmother's bones from Mexico City even if I'd found them. Buried almost a hundred years, who knows what shape they'd be in. And what would I tell the custom's officer when he asked what was in my gift bag from the National Museum of Anthropology? Tequila? Not likely.

Those bones wouldn't be easy to disguise, no matter how invisible my Scottish grandmother may have been in my life. Invisible? Maybe not the right word here. Present is better. She wasn't present in my life, but then, from what my mother tells me, she wasn't present in hers much either. A grandmother who left few traces of herself—who died before I had a chance to be born.

A few bones would be welcome, just to know she really did exist. Yet she must have. I have her genes. So did Mother. My bones are hers. So in a certain way, I did bring home her bones after all.

Except for the stories Mother told me over the years, only a single photograph of Grandmother remains, the only evidence she once existed. In it she's holding her first and oldest child on her lap; he's wearing a white christening gown. Scowling, he looks resigned to his fate. She looks absolutely bored with being part of this event and with the whole business of motherhood. Bored and removed. Her glance doesn't meet the camera's searching eye.

I wish I could say she looked murderous, another Medusa, but that would call for more emotion than she projects. Clearly, she had checked out already, and it wasn't long before she actually took off for Mexico City—in the mid-20s.

I had thought of visiting there many times over the years, hoping to catch a glimpse of her wandering the countryside, planting heather in that dry forbidding soil, but something held me back. It was easy to convince myself it wasn't safe for a woman to visit Mexico City alone; I was waiting until I had a companion who would join me. Besides, the travel warnings stressed the negatives: banditos attacking people traveling in cabs or even accosting them on the street and spiriting them away, demanding ransoms.

What had it been like when my grandmother moved there? Had a Mexican captured her so she couldn't return to her family? It would be nice to think so. How else can I explain what she did? She left Portree, Isle of Skye, after WWI ended to join her husband, a Scottish schoolmaster, in Canada. He'd gone to the new world before the war to find a better life for all of them. Seven years later, she and the children joined him, arriving in Calgary during a snowstorm.

To go from the warmth of the family womb in Portree (uncles, aunts, cousins, friends), a charming village, to this frigid climate on the barren prairies, must have been a jolt. Was it revenge at being forced to leave her home that encouraged her to leave husband and kids after a year and find work for herself with a family in the Mount Royal district? She must have been furious with my grandfather for making her join him. He was also a difficult man, his tongue stinging as much as his slaps. She refused to tolerate his abuse any longer.

In the 1920s, it took guts and daring for a woman to abandon her husband and kids. It took even greater nerve to travel to Mexico City with

# Poetry As A Tool of Inquiry

The image betrays us, leaving
in its wake a rush
of sound
and the fatal attraction that metaphor has

for poets. I'm not a conveyor belt, waiting
for the next word
to appear.
But when it does I'm relieved

to have something to cling to, a buoy
in this sea of language, a rudder
that will help me
find my way. Enough about words and all

their flaws. They bring life and so much
more, the bleakness
of their spare
surfaces, the aches and groans we associate

with cunning. Even oranges have that hush
to them, a reverence we save
for nature and
her creatures. Speaking propels us into space.


All that rhythm coagulates and convenes,
releasing a surge
of sound, rapture
to the ears, a hobbit hole we descend.

Chiron the Centaur paces, waiting
to be released.

*Lily Iona Mackenzie*

her lover, her employer. Did she know then she would never return to either Canada or her homeland?

Some might claim she had a psychotic break, but I think this interpretation is too clinical. Menopause madness? More plausible. But why do we need to assert a woman is mad or unbalanced if she chooses to leave her kids and an inattentive, abusive husband? Some children drive their parents to drink. Some aren't lovable. What if she just got fed up with the whole mess and wanted a life for herself before it was too late?

Or did she have a premonition of dying young (four years after she arrived in Mexico) and decided to do as much living as she could in the meantime? The city would have been much smaller then, only about a million people, and beautiful colonial buildings dominated, creating a European ambiance. It combined aspects of a world-class city with the Mexican village, the Zocalo the central focus, residents gathering at the huge plaza at the end of the day and strolling, men traveling in one direction, women in the other. Did she join this promenade, flashing her peasant skirt at a passing caballero?

When I arrived in Mexico City, eighty-five years later, I thought I would be overwhelmed. I was sure my grandmother's spirit would rise up and impress its image on me, as the Virgin of Guadalupe is reported to have done to the poor peasant Juan Diego when he had a vision of her. Surely my grandmother would make contact with a granddaughter who had come so far to find her.

But she didn't. Not even in my dreams. Or maybe I wasn't receptive enough to her presence. There's that word again: why would she be present for me if she weren't present for my mother and her four sons, five kids altogether. She gave birth to them. She did her duty by bringing them into the world. Surely they didn't expect her to raise them as well.

Everywhere I went in Mexico City, I expected to see her, serving me in a cafe, cleaning our hotel room, strolling across the Zocalo. I inquired about where I'd find death records, but the bureaucratic maze and lack of Spanish language skills discouraged me. It would take days and many pesos to make any headway. Even then, the chances of finding her grave seemed very slim. But I couldn't help wonder if she too had seen the Pyramids of the Sun and Moon. Had she marveled at their image rising out of the Mexico landscape? Did she climb the Pyramid of the Sun where she could she see for miles, the mountains looming in the distance?

I imagine her poised for flight, a quetzal, or something equally exotic, released from earthly concerns. At that height the breath labors, and the heart flutters, and she must have felt a kinship

with the dead sacrificed there, given one final view of all they were to lose at the flash of a knife. Maybe she waited for Mexico City's Angel of Independence to rescue her, or even the Aztec warrior, frozen in statue form on a main boulevard. Or perhaps Diana, another statue, a naked warrior woman who surely wouldn't let her die.

26

# Resurrection

*Lily Iona Mackenzie*

It ended not in the way marriages usually end. No divorce. No removal of rings. Not even any discord. We continued living in the same house. We slept in the same bed. We even had sex at times.

But the marriage had died and refused to be resurrected. Or maybe it couldn't be resurrected. Perhaps there is no afterlife; we're given only one chance. If we blow it, that's it.

◊

I awaken one morning. It's June, the time for weddings—new life, promise and hope. A glorious day, even for Northern California, sun in command, the sky a Mediterranean blue, a touch of cloud here and there to add tension—a day to die for.

I roll over and stare for a while at Don sleeping next to me. At other times I've felt proud ownership and warmth when I've watched him sleep, his arm flung over his head, dark curls tinged with gray growing erratically, mustache framing his lips, calling attention to their softness in the midst of all that bristle.

I want to kiss those lips, to explore their texture, but now they seem so foreign, lips of a stranger, hard, resisting, barring me from tasting the dark interior of his mouth. Still, I try to probe gently with my tongue, attempting to get past this barrier, searching for the pearl at the heart of the shell. I want to pry open these lips, force my way in.

He awakens like someone who's been under water, his mouth and lungs filling, flailing his arms, trying to catch his breath. His lids open, startled brown eyes registering fear. "What in hell are you doing, Brenda?"

He pushes me away and sits up in bed, wearing only his pajama bottoms. He used to wear only his tops. Now he seems to be protecting something.

"Christ, I thought I was having a nightmare. Shit." He shakes his head like a swimmer flicking water from his hair. "You scared the hell outta me."

I write my name on his bare back, circumnavigating the moles. He shrugs me off. "Stop. I don't feel like fooling around."

"I could help you get it up."

"Lay off, Brenda. I'm not in the mood."

He used to be in the mood. All the time. Much more than I was. I sing "Mr. Watcha call him watcha doing tonight. Hope you're in the mood and that you're feelin' all right...." Before he would join me, the two of us doing a kind of jig around the maypole of our bed. Not any more. Not since....

◊

It had been another splendid summer day. We'd just dropped off Don's mother at the rest home after taking her out for lunch and for a drive in my new VW Passat. The car radio was playing "Mac the Knife," and we were singing "Oh those sharks babe, have such teeth babe...." While reaching into the back seat for my purse, I pulled onto the freeway. Then the lights went out.

When I came to, I was in the hospital on a gurney, my only sister Stella holding my hand. I tried to sit up, but a piercing pain in my ribs stopped me. "Christ," I gasped. "What happened? Where's Don?"

"It's okay, Brenda. You've just got a few broken ribs. Don's in surgery. Head injury."

Worse than the pain in my ribs was the anguish that rushed through me: I'd been driving.

## The Art of Zen

Roof rats have invaded our attic, burrowing
into insulation and storage boxes, making
a home for their young. Whenever I open

the attic door their scat showers me
and the musky rodent smell seeps

into the house. It's zen
not to be attached
to our belongings.

Maybe they're a test of how ready
I am to let go

of something I can't take
with me. A 4.5 earthquake hit
yesterday and reminded me

of how tentative all this wood is
we call home. A little stronger

and we may have been sleeping
outside. The rats would take over
the demolished structure, creeping

at night through crevices and caves
left by the quake, noses twitching,

eyes glinting, claiming the destruction
as their own.

*Lily Iona Mackenzie*

If Don died, it was my fault. How could I live with myself?

As if reading my mind, Stella said, "It wasn't your fault. Some jerk in an SUV cut you off. The crash was unavoidable."

I wanted to believe her, but what if I'd been paying full attention to my driving? What if I hadn't reached for my purse? Could I have avoided the accident?

I'll never know.

"Mrs. MacLeod?" My name. I looked around. A man in his mid-forties, my age, wearing green scrubs, stood over me and rested his hand on mine. "You're husband will be okay. We had to put a plate in his head, but he's lucky to be alive."

Lucky to be alive. Plate in his head. My Don?

"Don't worry. He'll be good as new in no time." The doctor smiled down at me, the smile not quite reaching his eyes.

◊

Well, Don did recover, that's true, though I wouldn't call him "good as new." Someone with a plate in his head will never be good as new. I just hope he doesn't get close to any giant magnets. Most important, he was alive. I guess I should say he *is* alive. Sort of.  So little of the man I married remains that at times it seems like he did die. It's not easy sharing a bed or a house with a stranger, believe me. Or a ghost.

It took months for him to regain his strength, and even longer to recover his memories, the part of his brain that was most seriously damaged. He never did recoup everything. His past resembles Swiss cheese. We spend a lot of time nibbling around the holes, trying to piece together his life for him.

It wasn't so bad during his recuperation. There was still hope my husband would turn up eventually, wiggling through those gaps in his synapses. Occasionally I'd get a glimpse of the man I married, his humor almost surfacing, but it was like a flickering candle in a drafty room. It didn't take much to snuff it out. I assumed these lapses were just part of the healing process and soon everything would be as before.

But it became harder to keep hoping. Everything about Don seemed different, except for his appearance, though the surgery had left a purple scar near his receding hairline. The angry color gradually faded somewhat, but the scar was a constant reminder of my carelessness. Each time I looked at him, I felt like I'd been kicked in the stomach.

◊

In the past, Don was indifferent to what went into the food he ate, consuming whatever I put on his plate, willing to eat almost anything. But after the accident, he became obsessed with his diet, insisting on shopping at Whole Foods rather than Safeway. "Organic's the only way to go" became his constant mantra, though in the past he pooh poohed organic hunters. He'd say, "I like the feeling of Safeway better. No yuppies there trying to show off how superior they are." Yeah, right.

Scene: breakfast. Don's sitting in our nook. He's begun his granola rant for the morning. He has several bowls lined up in front of him, each offering a different variation of the cereal. He puts a spoonful of one kind in his mouth, checking the crunch level, swirling it around like some rare wine before swallowing and moving on to the next bowl. "That one has a little almond flavor," he says, nudging my arm and pointing, "but it overpowers the other ingredients."

I nod, trying to read the *Times*, poking my spoon into the Rice Crispies I bought at Safeway. Granola requires too much effort to eat. All that crunch. It takes forever to work your way through a bowl. But Don thrives on the stuff, enjoying the endless chewing each spoonful requires. He even closes his eyes as he munches, shutting out all distractions, unaware of my snap, crackle, and pop.

If I get up and clear the table, put dishes in the dishwasher, sweep the floor, he sulks. "Christ, Brenda, can't you do that later? It's no fun talking to a wall." He expects me to sit through this ordeal, needing an audience for his pronouncements about the merits of granola sweetened with honey versus ones using only fruit juice, expounding on the crunch and the relative quality of each kind.

Before the accident, he read the *Times* too, and we talked about politics and what was happening in the world. Now he has no interest in reading anything, except for the ingredients in the food he buys.

These fixations aren't limited to food but to every aspect of our life together. He even needs to discuss the merits of high-octane over low-octane gas. I don't even know what an octane is. All I can think of is octave, an octave of gas. I told him, "I don't give a damn about what kind of gas you buy." We were having dinner, and I just couldn't get into a conversation about gas. I stared at the peas swimming in a sea of soup. They looked like bullets to me, and I wanted to plug him with one, anything to shut him up.

But I'm afraid it would have taken more than a bullet to do that. He just kept his rant going, lecturing me on octane: "Octane's the fuel's resistance to knocking. There's no benefit if the octane's higher than what the engine needs.

29

Engine knock occurs when fuel in a combustion chamber ignites before it should. This disrupts the engine's operation. But electronic knock sensors are now common and have nearly eliminated engine disruption. So you don't need high octane gas any more."

"No kidding," I say. "What a relief that is."

Of course, that wasn't the end to his lecture on gas. He kept it up for days. I was ready to run screaming from the house.

His next subject? The virtues of various types of toilet paper. Double versus single ply. Colored versus white. Recycled versus non-recycled paper. He filibustered for days on that one. I wanted to stuff his mouth with a roll to shut him up and get some peace. I feel I'll scream if I have to listen to more of his analysis.

What kind of monster did the surgeon release? I mentioned my concerns to Don's doctor once, but he brushed them off. "There's always an adjustment period after this kind of surgery, Mrs. McLeod. Be patient. You're lucky your husband's alive." Thanks a lot, doc. Plunge the knife a little deeper, why don't you. I should just wear a sign "I'M GUILTY" like Hester Prynne. Except I'd sooner be branded an adulteress than carry around this guilt for essentially murdering my husband.

◊

Anyway, I don't feel lucky. I resemble Chicken Little, only for me the sky *has* fallen and I keep getting hit with chunks of it. To make it worse, I'm truly chicken. I don't want to deal with this new husband. I want the old one back. But I'm stuck with the chains of marriage. How can I just check out?

My daughters would disown me for running out on their father in his time of need, and I wouldn't be able to live with myself. But they don't have to live with him. I do. They're both in college in another state. They saw him after his surgery. Otherwise, they come home rarely for short visits. They haven't really experienced the new Don.

Catch 22? Hell is more accurate. I couldn't have lived with myself if he'd died, and I'm having trouble living with him—or myself—because he lived.

The situation might be more bearable if Don's job took him away for several hours a day, but he has his own PR business. And guess what. He runs it out of our house. I'm his assistant, so I'm blessed with his presence round the clock. Prior to the accident, I was Don's partner, not an assistant. Now I'm completely under his thumb.

Scene: After the granola rant, Don says, "We'd better get to work." Of course, he doesn't take into consideration that the house is also my work. Before the crash, he shared most of the chores with me. Not any more, unless you count his grocery shopping, which doesn't amount to much since he only buys his current obsessions, not all the items needed to keep a household going. So I shop, too.

I say, "Give me a hand clearing the dishes, hon."

"No time. I have to dictate a bunch of letters, and there are some phone calls you need to make for me. Time to generate new business!"

"But I'm in the middle of the big project you gave me yesterday. You said you needed *IT* pronto."

"That can wait. This is more important."
I bite my tongue. Instead of saying up yours, buster, I make excuses for him. He's still adjusting

to life post-surgery. He's still finding himself. He'll mellow over time.

But at the moment, he's a tyrant, my employer *and* my husband. Before I would have said "Buzz off, Bozo" if he got too bossy, and we would have laughed over it. Now—you've got it: The guilt's sucking the life from me and giving him too much power.

I understand how Prometheus felt, enduring his punishment, strapped to a rock, an eagle eating his liver every day. All I stole was Don's former life, but there seems no end in sight for me either.

◊

Who is this new man I share a bed with? Has he always been there in the shadows but I've been too naïve or blind to notice? Of course, he's totally unaware of what I'm feeling. Or totally indifferent. Maybe he always has been and I just ignored it.

I try to block out the present with the past, thinking about our former life together. I remember after Kay, our first daughter, was born. We were only in our early 20's, barely adults. We didn't have a clue about caring for a baby. I was the youngest in my family, so I had no experience raising younger siblings. He was an only child. But we learned fast. Still, it killed me that Don was more skilled at changing diapers than I was. We used cloth ones then. They had to be folded into a triangle and secured with big safety pins. His always looked so neat; mine barely stayed on her bottom.

Were we really happy once, zipping along, anticipating our daughters being launched and helping each other through old age? Maybe I'm inventing that part of our life. If the past exists only in memory and artifacts, and if memory dies with a person, then maybe there isn't such a thing as a past. Besides, how do I know my memories aren't faulty, a defense against what's going on at the moment? Anyway, the new Don keeps intruding into these reminiscences, making it impossible to escape him, robbing me even of those earlier, more carefree times.

Worse, everything in this house reminds me of what has died in our marriage. I can't go into a room without being inundated by evoked images. Don and I bought the Shaker chair several years ago during a trip to New England, drawn to its simple upright lines, even though its origins in a strict religious community gave it a strait-laced quality. We christened the chair Martha soon after we got it home, trying out several positions on it, trying to shake its celibate vibes. Martha has kept watch over our family since then.

Then there's the lamp that has a mermaid for a base; we found it at a garage sale our first year together. Her green nipples light up whenever the lamp's turned on, and she has a dusky rose lampshade, fringed with six-inch tassels. We paid $1.00 for it and giggled all the way home, wondering what Don's mother would say when she saw those lit-up nipples in our living room. We thought she'd be shocked.

She wasn't; she loved it. So when I look at the mermaid, I see Don's mother and my mother and my daughters. It also reminds me of mermaids surfacing from the depths and life's mysteries.

Every item has a similar story, though now these objects have taken on their own life and seem to be mocking me rather than giving comfort as they once did. Actually, my whole marriage has become a mockery. Resembling Medusa's head, the tendrils reach out and entangle me. Like Medusa, I may have to destroy something precious to me for my own survival.

A marriage can and does form a third entity, something beyond the control of the couple involved, a life of its own. Like a leech, it can suck the vitality from husband and wife, feeding off of them for its own survival. I'm not talking about all marriages. Only the ones that turn bad, like rotten fruit, stinking up the place and exacting a price for their continued existence.

◊

Whenever Don's napping or shopping, I get out of the house. I've been attending an art therapy workshop that meets three times a week. It's such a relief not to talk if I don't want to. Nor do I need to listen if others blab on. If people do talk, they do it quietly, as if we're in a library, respectful of others' space. We're all there to focus on the art materials. Period.

It isn't that I'm trying to make a sculpture or anything. In fact, I try very hard not to make art at all. I only want the clay to surrender to my fingers probing, to experience its malleability, to be soothed by its sensuous texture. It's therapeutic just to have a little control over something. But most of the time, I surrender to it, letting the clay lead.

Stan, the teacher, doesn't do a lot of teaching, thank god. He looks totally out of place in that setting with his broad shoulders, great pecs, and bulging quads and biceps. He must have been a football player in another life. He drifts from person to person, grunting when he sees something that pleases him, silent most of the time.

I didn't get it at first when he seemed to linger at my table much longer than at the others. Since the accident, I've lost any sense of myself as sexually desirable, so the thought he might find me attractive never entered my mind. Imagine my surprise when this hunk started breathing heavily while standing next to me, this raw animal energy bouncing off his skin. He even started loading up on after-shave before class, a mating call for him, I guess, but a real turn off for me.

He's not my type. Seriously not. I've always gone for the slender, poetic looking guys. Like Don when he was younger. But it's still flattering to have a man without holes in his mind showing interest in little ole me. I find myself responding to the pure animal vibration Stan gives off, even though I try to ignore him.

Most of the time, I let my mind go blank and sit there, the lump of terracotta plopped on a piece of board resting on my lap. Then I knead and push it for two hours, pressing it away from my body, working with the heels of my hands until the clay finally fits the square wood surface its resting on. And that's all I do, each day emptying myself of something distasteful. It's the best therapy I've ever had.

But I can't go on like this. Don is so absorbed in his own world (he just spent days raving about birdfeed, claiming that the quality isn't as good as it once was) that he doesn't even notice I'm totally miserable. I want to feel sorry for him and embrace his new limitations—his blindness. I want to make his life easier.

I can't.

Till death us do part repeats over and over in my mind. I've made a vow. A promise is a promise. I can't take a lover. That would just give me a bigger load of guilt to cart around. And I can't run out on a crip. Can I?

But what if Don were to run out on me? I wouldn't be responsible then. It would be his choice. Maybe he'll meet someone who'll actually fall for this new Don. He's not a bad looking guy. A little paunch. Not unusual for someone his age. He still has his hair. Earns a decent living. A pretty good catch given the scarcity of eligible heterosexual men in the Bay Area. He'd get nabbed fast.

And a new woman wouldn't have memories of former times to combat. She wouldn't know any different. She'd fall for the new Don. I even start sifting through my current women friends, wondering if I can do some matchmaking. Kathy, one of my more dippy acquaintances, might complement Don better than I do. But again my daughters come into the picture. They wouldn't stand for it. Nor would I. I wouldn't wish Kathy on anyone, especially Don. She has a brain the size of a peanut.

◊

I decide if I can't get rid of Don himself, I can start moving in a new direction. I want to shed some of the things we purchased together during those halcyon times: it's simply too painful to look at them day in and day out. So I hold a yard sale one weekend when Don is off scouting a band that needs his PR skills. It's his first trip alone since the accident, a major step for him—and for me. He needs to know he can do things on his own without me as an appendage. I need to know I can have a life without him. It's our only hope as a couple. Independence.

Actually, I don't have a yard sale exactly; it's a household furnishings' sale, the yard part being a teaser. I put an ad in the newspaper under yard sales. I also post notices on all the telephone poles in the neighborhood. Then I put a few things outside as a come on and invite people inside. "Take a look," I say. "Make me an offer I can't refuse."

Some of my neighbors turn up, of course, sniffing around. Sally from next door climbs through the bushes separating our properties, pushing away cobwebs. "You and Don moving?"

I say no.

"You're not breaking up I hope. Not after all you've been through together." Her face scrunches up with worry.

"Nope. We just need to clear out the clutter."

She makes an offer for our mermaid, but I don't want the lamp moving next door where I can see it all the time. I'm relieved when a stranger, a pint-sized male, bids higher. In the middle of this bidding war, my heart lurches around in my chest. I'm more attached emotionally to the mermaid than I am to the new Don. I choke back the tears and shout "Sold to the man in the green sweat outfit."

As much as I hate to see the mermaid go, I make a sizable amount more than the $1.00 we paid for her. I do well on the other items too. What has been junk to us is a new category—distressed, or antique.

By Sunday night, the place is practically empty, dust balls chasing each other around the bare wooden floors. I even managed to sell the rugs. I'm feeling empty myself, wrung out from the experience of giving up these treasures Don and I had discovered together. The only thing left is Martha, our Shaker chair, the one thing I absolutely couldn't part with, and Don's favorite black leather recliner—I didn't have the heart to let that go, though I did get a good offer for it. I also didn't touch the girls' rooms or the computers. But the rest? Gone.

And I've pocketed the money. It's tempting to pack a couple of suitcases and buy a plane ticket to Costa Rica or Puerto Vallarta. Start a new life. It's so tempting that I even check out what Expedia.com has to offer. But I keep getting flooded with images of Don and me and the girls. Their first communion. The recitals and dance performances. I remember Don attending Lamaze with me, and he was such a rock during both births: he was excellent with the breathing exercises and coached me so well during labor that the time flew by. He never left my side.

I've been trying to blot out the past, to prevent it from bleeding into the present, unwilling to let the two merge. But the past does exist; it isn't just hitched to our possessions. It shifts and changes as we do, our present coloring everything. I've also been unwilling to explore what this new Don has to offer me, forgetting that the man I married is still lurking somewhere inside him. I've kept him away and let my guilt turn him into a tyrant.

◊

I just had a déjà vu feeling that I've had this experience before of sitting in a practically empty house, waiting for Don to return. And in fact I have. When we first bought this place, we couldn't afford much furniture, but we didn't care. We had a bed, a dresser, a kitchen table and chairs, adding

34

what we could from yard sales or flea markets when we got a good deal.

He didn't have his own PR business then but worked for someone else, gone all day. I was a full-time mother with two toddlers under foot all day, just a year a part. I loved the girls. Don't get me wrong. But by the end of the day, I wanted an adult to talk to who could use complete sentences and wasn't just focusing on me, me, me. Know what I mean?

So when I heard his car pull into the driveway, my heart soared. I was elated to see him walk through the doorway. He gave me a lop-sided smile that I loved so much, tossed his briefcase on a folding chair, and said, "Baby," wrapping me in his arms, the word echoing throughout the house. The girls tottered into the room and squealed, grabbing his legs.

You can see why it isn't so easy to fracture a family and be responsible for radically changing everyone's life. I have a writer friend who does that with her characters. She can invent whatever past or future she desires for her creations, not having to bear the consequences. But we aren't characters in a work of fiction. We have to live with our choices. My daughters: it would hit them the hardest. They wouldn't have a history they could trust. Their childhood would seem like a deception. It would throw their whole identities into question. How could I live with doing that to them?

Not that marriages shouldn't or don't end. People grow apart. Maybe the split in Don's and my relationship *is* permanent and the girls will just have to adjust, as I've had to adjust since the accident. I can't protect them forever.

I'm sitting on Martha, waiting for Don to return from his trip, and I'm thinking about resurrection. I've never quite believed the stories of Jesus resurrecting from the dead. Not only does it seem physically impossible, but it also makes a statement about heaven itself. If it were so great, then why in hell would Jesus return to this mundane life? I don't quite buy it that he sacrificed heaven for us. Besides, I'm not Jesus, willing to forfeit what's left of my life for the good of—what?

I'm mulling these things when Don walks in the door, suitcase in one hand, briefcase in the other. I thought he'd throw a fit when he saw our furnishings were gone, maybe even turn violent. So I'm surprised at the look of relief that passes over his face, as if a dark cloud has lifted. He's wearing a fedora that hides the scar, allowing me to forget for a moment the accident even happened, and he's shaved off his mustache.

"Hey," he says, "you've been housecleaning." I nod.
"I hated that old stuff. Just never had the nerve to say so."
Our voices echo in the empty room. The reverberations whack us around a bit, like a Zen koan, throwing us back on ourselves. Maybe something *can* rise from the dead. Resurrection may not come in the form we expect. It may not come at all. But it's worth giving it a chance.

For more information on our spotlight author, please visit her blog at:
lilyionamackenzie.wordpress.com

# Fight or Flight

*By Philip Hoy*

Evelyn's purse began to vibrate in her lap again. Her phone had been going off all morning. She knew who it was. Mr. Schwartz was standing only two desks away, but he had his back to her, explaining something to Luis. He would be a while.

"Hey. Why won't you return my text?"

It was Mark. Evelyn looked up from her purse. Schwartz was still explaining.

She switched the pencil to her left hand and began thumbing the keys on the phone in her purse with her right, "I'm in class."

"I've been texting you all morning."

"I'm in class."

"You didn't call me back last night."

Schwartz was now leaning heavily on Luis's desk with one hand and gesturing in the air with the other, his hand fluttering as he spoke like a one-winged bird. "My mom was mad I got back so late."

"Did she take your phone?"

"No."

"Why didn't you call me back then?"

Her thumb twitched once, but remained hovering above the keys. Wasn't it obvious? Did she have to spell it out for him?

The phone vibrated again, but she was no longer holding it. Her hand had drifted up toward her face and her fingertips pressed lightly to her lips, remembering...

"I'll try not to be home too late," Evelyn said, slinging her back pack over her shoulder and opening the back kitchen door. She told her mother she was going to her friend's house to study, but just to be on the safe side, she had done the dinner dishes before she asked. Jennifer's parents were out of town and wouldn't be back until tomorrow.

"You're walking?" her mother asked, looking up from her ironing.

"She only lives two streets over, Mom." Evelyn considered offering to iron her dad's work uniforms, but that might have made her mom suspicious.

Her mother frowned past her at the purpling sky outside.

"Can you believe he's giving us another test already?" Evelyn complained, as if in response to her mother's concern for the time, "I mean, we just had a test on Monday."

"And you're going over there dressed in that?" her mother asked, eyeing the baggy sweat pants, sandals, and old t-shirt Evelyn was wearing.

"Mom, it's just Jennifer's."

"And is that brother of hers going to be there? The football player. What's his name?"

"Oh please, mother, he has a girl friend."

"Hmm. You better make sure you're just studying."

"We are mother, I promise," she said, stepping outside and closing the door before her mother had time to change her mind.

Evelyn stopped on the dark side of the house, where her dad kept the trash cans, to pull off the sweats and t-shirt and stuff them into her back-pack. Underneath, she was wearing the black tank-top dress Jennifer had loaned her. "Robert won't be able to resist you!" Jennifer had declared the night before, "You have to wear it to my party!" Evelyn smoothed the wrinkles as best she could from the front of the skirt, shoved the back-pack between two trash cans, and slipped out the side gate.

"And you're positive he's coming?" Evelyn had asked Jennifer.

"For the hundredth time, yes," Jennifer had said, "We've been texting each other all day."

"All day? I don't even have his number."

"Well, it's not right for me to give it to you, he has to do it."

Evelyn could hear the thump of music coming from inside Jennifer's house as she walked up the driveway. The garage door was open, but it was dark inside so she tried the front door instead. It was unlocked. Sounds of talking and laughing were coming from the kitchen. Jennifer's voice was the loudest, but Evelyn thought she recognized Robert's laugh in the mix.

The brightly lit kitchen was crowded with people. "Evelyn!" Jennifer shouted as she entered the room.

"Evelyn!" the crowd echoed as everyone turned to stare at her.

"To Evelyn!" Jennifer said loudly, lifting her drink high in the air with one arm. The other was wrapped tightly around Robert's waist.

"To Evelyn!" shouted Robert along with the rest, his arm wrapped just as tightly around Jennifer. They all drank.

"You wore my dress!" Jennifer screeched, as if Evelyn had surprised her with a gift of flowers. "It looks good on you! Doesn't she look good, Robert?"

Evelyn turned and flew from the room before Robert – or anyone else – had a chance to answer. The nearest way out was the back door leading to the garage. She rushed through it, slammed it shut behind her, and ran straight into Jennifer's brother, Mark.

"Evelyn?"

"Evelyn?" Mr. Schwartz was standing in the front of the class. "What do you think, Evelyn?" Everyone had turned to look at her. "We're talking about the symbolism of the forest in the story. You looked like you had something important to say."

Evelyn knew this was Schwartz's way of telling her to pay attention. "The forest?" she repeated, and her purse vibrated in her lap.

"Yes, the one in the book that you have open in front of you on your desk."

Evelyn looked down at her notes from the day before, "Fear... of... the... unknown?"

"O...kay," he said, sounding a little disappointed, "Yes, but what else? How does the forest contrast with the town?"

"No rules?" someone said.

"Yes, okay," Schwartz shifted his attention to the other side of the room, "In the forest, the same rules don't apply, right?"

Evelyn chanced a look at her phone. "Stop ignoring me!" it read.

She dropped her hand into her purse again and thumbed a response, "I'm in class!"

"I'll be waiting for you outside."

"Whoa, hey, Evelyn, where're you going?" Mark asked, not moving out of her way.

"Home," she said, trying to push past him.

"But you just got here."

"She's always doing things like this to me!" Evelyn shouted. "I don't even know why we're friends!" And then she started crying. "How can you even put up with her?" she sobbed.

"Who else is going to take care of her?" he asked.

She let Mark guide her over to the old couch against the wall in the garage. He disappeared for a second and returned with a large white handkerchief, handing it to Evelyn. She wiped her eyes and nose with it before she realized he'd given her a t-shirt.

"Don't worry," he said, gesturing to the washer and dryer against the opposite wall, "I got it from the clean pile."

"Sorry."

"Hey, it's okay. Mind if I sit?"

She shrugged. Mark took this for a yes and sat down next to her on the couch. The garage wasn't as dark from the inside as it first seemed. The glow from the street lights gave a silvery outline to the objects around her, including Mark. She realized he had probably watched her walk up the driveway just minutes earlier.

"Not what you expected, huh?"

"You know, it's not really my scene," she said, trying to laugh.

He chuckled at that, "I can dig what you're saying, sister."

"And you? Why aren't you in there?"

"Aw, you know," he said, making his voice as deep as possible, "I'm trying to watch my figure," and he leaned toward Evelyn a little and flexed his muscled arm.

Evelyn felt her eyes widen.

His face broke into an embarrassed grin and for a moment he looked just like a little boy.

Evelyn could feel her own face grow suddenly warm.

Neither one spoke for what seemed like minutes, but then, before she could stop herself, Evelyn asked, "So, where's your girlfriend?"

"Stacy? She couldn't get out. You know, school night and all."

"Yeah, I know."

There was more uncomfortable silence.

Evelyn searched for some other topic – anything besides Mark's girlfriend, but her mind was filled suddenly with the memory of the day about a month ago when Mark and Stacy were walking in front of her on their way to class. She wasn't trying to stalk them, but when she got to her own class, she just looked straight ahead and kept walking after them. Stacy was wearing his lettermen's jacket. He was carrying her books. They were holding hands. Mark and Stacy: the football star and the cheerleader. Talk about a cliché. It would be pathetic if they didn't look so good together.

The couple stopped suddenly in front of the open door of a class room and Mark pulled Stacy toward him for a kiss. Without thinking, Evelyn shifted her back pack to one side and let it hit Stacy hard on the shoulder as she hurried past them. She heard Stacy's muffled complaint behind her as she let the crowd carry her around the next corner.

On an adrenaline surge of guilty excitement, she hurried back to her own class. She hadn't told anyone about that day, not even Jennifer.

Not sure what exactly would come out, she opened her mouth and said, "Have you read The Scarlet Letter?"

"The what?"

"The Scarlet Letter. You know, the girl has to wear a big A on her chest and the minister can't admit he's the father."

"Oh yeah, Shwartz's class. With the wild little girl in the forest."

"Yeah, we're reading it right now."

"Have you made it to the part where the little girl is throwing rocks at the seagulls?"

"I'm not sure—"

"Really?" Mark asked, sounding genuinely interested, "That's like my favorite part."

"Oh, she's like on the beach with her mom and her mom's talking with the Chillingworth dude?" They were little grey birds, actually. Not that it really mattered.

"Yeah, and the little girl—what's her name?"

"Pearl."

"Yeah, Pearl. Well she has this like wild streak in her right? And she starts throwing rocks at these birds, having fun, you know?"

"I think I remember." Of course she remembered, but she couldn't help wondering why Mark was so into that part of the story. Schwartz hadn't really even talked about it in class.

"Well, she hits one, and breaks its wing. And then the fun goes out of it because she realizes the birds and her are the same – both wild. Her mom's being punished for having her and her dad won't support her. I mean she's got a lot to be angry about – but she's not a bad person, she's not really mean. She's just a kid, you know?"

"Yeah, I never really thought of it that way." Evelyn could hear the steady pulse of music and the clamor of voices coming from inside the house. Her recent humiliation in the kitchen seemed so unimportant now.

"...with sudden... tenderness... she threw her... arms around him... and pressed..."

Oh no, thought Evelyn, we're reading? That man had no mercy what-so-ever! Now she would have to pay attention. And who was reading, anyway, Pita? She might as well be whispering.

Evelyn waved her hand in the air to get Mr. Schwartz's attention and then gestured desperately toward her ear.

"Lupita," he said, "a little louder, please."

There, that would convince Schwartz she was, "fully engaged," as he liked to say.

"...we are not... Hester... the worst sinners... in the... world... There is one ... worse..."

She placed her finger at the top of the next paragraph in case she was next to read, and with her other hand sent, "She'll see," on her phone to Mark.

"Her class is in 200's," he replied.

A car drove by and momentarily lit up the inside of the garage, causing the shadows to sway across the walls like branches in the wind. "What are you thinking," Mark asked her when it was dark again.

"That I lied to my mom to come here."

He turned to look at her.

"And you?" she said, "Tell me what you were thinking."

She felt his eyes on her face.

"When I was... ten, probably, I was playing with my friend in his back yard." He stopped, studying her face a moment before continuing. "We caught this pigeon. We snuck up on it and threw a sheet over it like a big net, like in the movies, you know? Well, it couldn't fly away, so it started running around the yard with the sheet over its head, dragging the cover around, bumping into things. It looked so funny. We were laughing so hard. 'Hold it! Hold it!' my friend started yelling so I stepped on the corner of the sheet. 'It's getting away!' I was yelling."

He was sitting with his hands between his knees, rubbing his palms together roughly as he spoke. "Then my friend picked up a brick, you know, the ones that go around like a flower garden, or whatever – I mean, he could barely lift it – and ran over and dropped it on the pigeon."

"Oh my God, what did you do?"

"We were still laughing, you know? It was like the pigeon wasn't even there any more – just the sheet... and then blood started to soak through the white – like this dark red spreading out... I just ran home. I didn't tell anyone."

"—oh."

She reached out with one hand and placed it over his. He stopped rubbing them together.

"Anyway," he said, and he turned and gave her one of his trademark, heartbreaker smiles, "that's what I was thinking."

His eyes, though. His eyes were still those of the ten year old boy in his story. She couldn't look away from them.

He took her hand between his.

She felt herself leaning toward him, like she was falling– falling in slow motion, and then the ground rushed up to meet her and she closed her eyes and let herself crash into him.

She was completely lost.

Now Luis was reading, "what we did had a con... se... cra... tion... of its own. We..."

She didn't even know what page she was supposed to be on.

She felt caged.

"Someone will tell," she texted back.

God! Why didn't Schwartz just take her phone away and put her out of her misery? Why couldn't Mark just leave her alone? Why couldn't they both just act like it didn't happen?

Her phone vibrated.

"I don't care," was his reply.

But it did happen.

And he was right outside.

Her hand shot up in the air.

"Mr. Schwartz!"

"Yes? Evelyn."

"May I please take the hall pass to go to the restroom?"

◆————————————————◆

# Sleep Clinic

Driving off orthogonals
A swirling color gradient
Sweeps from the plan on the screen
Is it just pretty I ask or
Does it mean something?
I'm designing a sleep clinic she says
You can see
Most of the space is dark
We part
Too late
Red lights wink
Lampposts sink in heaps
Of orange maple leaves
O yellowed moon you've aged
Your pages curl
Churlish of me to reminisce
Greener pastures true blue friends
I'll miss my exit
Too distracted
Turn up the rock
Roll on indigo
Car radio blistering
Violent Femmes
Let me go home
Wild violet night
Smack the black tarmac
Into shards of night
It's mostly black she says
Relaxing
Just this piece has color, she points
On the corner of the screen
A spectrum smokes.
So patients can, you know, sleep

*Barbara Lowenthal*

# Love is a Dirty Word

*Samuel Fry*

When I think I have feelings for a girl, the English language becomes ridiculous and unhelpful. The three words I can most nearly use to define what I feel are "like," "crush," and finally "love." The first two just don't say it, and 'love' I have to be careful with, because we tend to treat it like a dirty word.

If I were to scream "fuck" into the starry night sky with all my heart, it might be taken any number of different ways, just as the statement "I love you" might be received. To apply the word "love" newly to a romantic interest yields uncannily awkward and confusing results—like applying marshmallow whip to liquid mortar. I wish it wouldn't work out this way, but it would—at least to all budding romances. Which is why I have never used this word to describe my feelings toward the girls I have fallen in love with.

I can count on my fingers all the girls I've ever had feelings for, from grade school up to now—without equivocation: Claire, Nora, Posey, Belinda, Lyndie, Kelly, and Autumn. Posey was "the one that got away," Kelly was just my misjudgment, and Belinda I'll never live down—I decided I wasn't emotionally ready. The rest don't matter, except now—except for Autumn—and she's the one that "love" becomes very dirty for, even if I do, in some sense or another, love her completely.

Love never works, for the "now" romance. The experience itself is a sliding scale, and the more in love we are, the more reality turns into fantasy—just the same way it would for a pilot of an aircraft heading into the Bermuda Triangle. As soon as we determine who we love, the word is never enough. And, by some peculiar irony, the listener will receive the word too much, and too little the feeling behind it. They will hear it loaded and blast into their own personal bubble, and it will rip their fucking world apart. When they realize they have survived a shotgun spray, they will ask the shooter to kindly take aim at themselves before harming others. Such is often the story for our ill-thought-out affections.

When I think about Autumn, the traditional three words in my arsenal of romantic feelings cease to matter, let alone exist. I would rather lie to her about anything else than my feelings for her, which is why I take the time to write this at all. For her, "like," "crush," and "love" become lost figments of cloud in the sky of my heart. So arbitrary the name for the feelings—the feeling like my face is irradiated by a massive sunbeam when I see her walk toward me; the feeling like my stomach is falling down a melting set of stairs when she walks away—I will call it "Carlos" from here on out.

My heart sings Carlos out into the far reaches of the earth every time I catch a glimpse of her face, her hair, her eyes, her wonderful little feet. And I'm reminded that while love is a dirty word—plaything of married couples and family members—my Carlos is a sacred and exhilarating phenomenon. Only I feel Carlos, because it is mutually exclusive to me. I define it, own it, and reserve it. So when I say I feel Carlos, right here and now—for Autumn, when I'm away from her—that's something special. Something I don't hesitate to share. What I am doing when I feel Carlos is I'm really feeling me.

Carlos is a part of my character—an abstraction clinging deep to the neurons in my brain and scribbling itself into my skull. Not even she could take it away.

She could ask me not to say dirty words, but she can't *ever* ask me to unfascine my mind from my head, and scoop away with an ice-cream spoon my present Carlos for her, nor my previous Carlos for the other six. The power to perform this operation rests with me, and frankly, I'd rather not. It sounds like it might be painful. Feelings are not forged to be unborn.

And what matters most is the feeling, not the word. For some, it might be Fred. Others, it might be Wilma. Who can say? I would rather run the Carlos banner high atop my castle than hide another minute behind an overused and over-tainted word which is best reserved for casual conversations only: father to son, mother to daughter, sister to brother. So long has love been the umbrella franchise for romance, leasing rights to movies, television, and any random schmooze between drunks in the night, that we have forgotten its very purpose as being unique unto each individual who feels it.

When it comes to love, we must be our own visionaries, and recuse misguided attempts to let the word itself tie up and torture our souls inside the prisons of traditional romantic paradigms. If love is dirty, it is because we have made it so.

Because it isn't a dirty *feeling*.

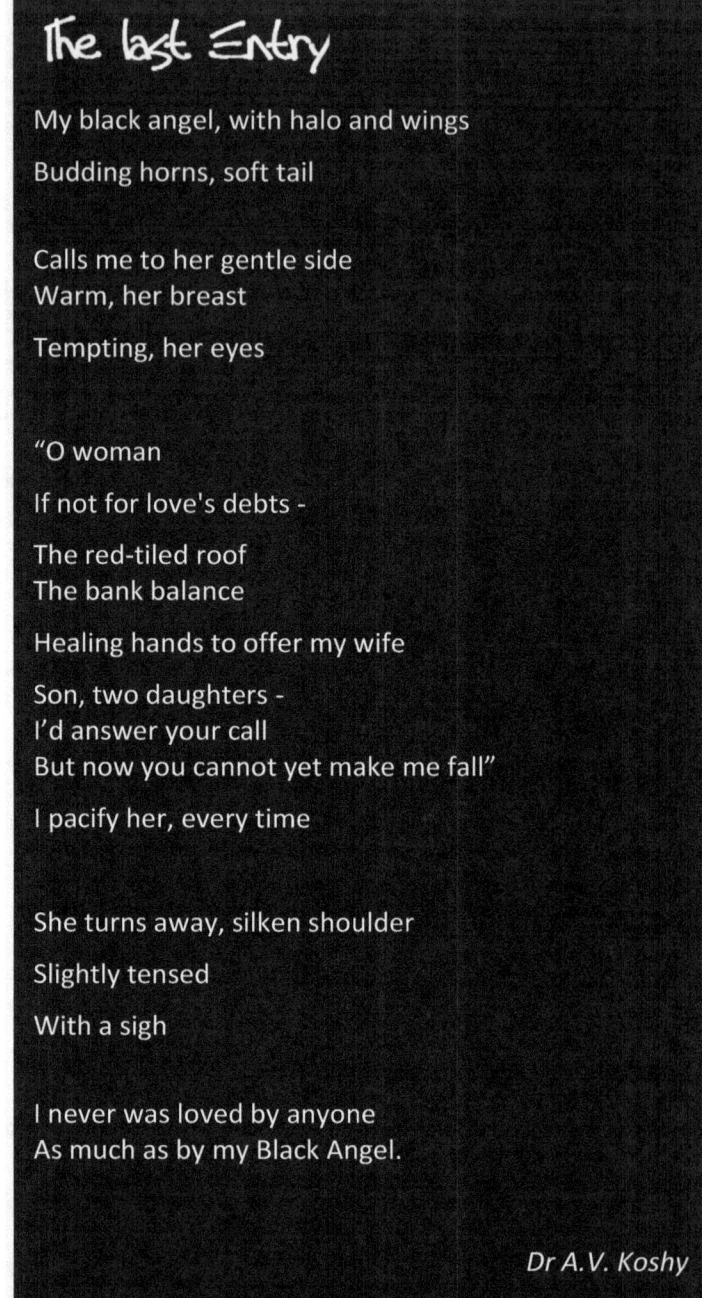

## The last Entry

My black angel, with halo and wings

Budding horns, soft tail

Calls me to her gentle side
Warm, her breast

Tempting, her eyes

"O woman

If not for love's debts -

The red-tiled roof
The bank balance

Healing hands to offer my wife

Son, two daughters -
I'd answer your call
But now you cannot yet make me fall"

I pacify her, every time

She turns away, silken shoulder

Slightly tensed

With a sigh

I never was loved by anyone
As much as by my Black Angel.

*Dr A.V. Koshy*

# Please! Where Are The Scissors?!?

*Harmoni McGlothlin*

"Adam you're going to love this," Bess grins, leaning into my window as I set my parking break. "The crazy bitch is at it again."

"Her official title is The Lunatic."

"Yeah, whatever," Bess Brown laughs without humor, exhaling a puff of bluish smoke off her non-filtered Camel. "You should see her sniffing around, chewing her nails and everything, asking everyone-- even Wheeler, for fucks sake!-- if they saw you take the scissors off her desk."

The Lunatic in question is the receptionist in the administrative office of Bridge Creek, our oh-so-exclusive retirement 'community' (not facility, never that) for elderly artists, journalists, award-winning writers, and their withered (but still wealthy) patrons.

Riddle me this: If half the 'residents' (not 'patients', don't even think that) at Bridge Creek can't hear and the other half can barely speak-- Why live (rot) among your peers? There is no chance of any actual, intellectual interaction.

I guess it's not about making sense. It's about making money and it's a hundred percent on that score. Bess could tell you all about that. She's the bookkeeper at Bridge Creek. I'm the Assistant Executive Director.

I blink at her, brow raised to balance a sideways smirk as I grab my bulging briefcase off the passenger's seat. The car door slams behind me as I follow Bess and her trailing cloud of smoke across the parking lot.

"Her damned scissors," Bess says, folding nicotine stained fingers over a mouthful of broken teeth. "Heard this song before? It's a friggin' classic."

Yeah, classic is the word alright.

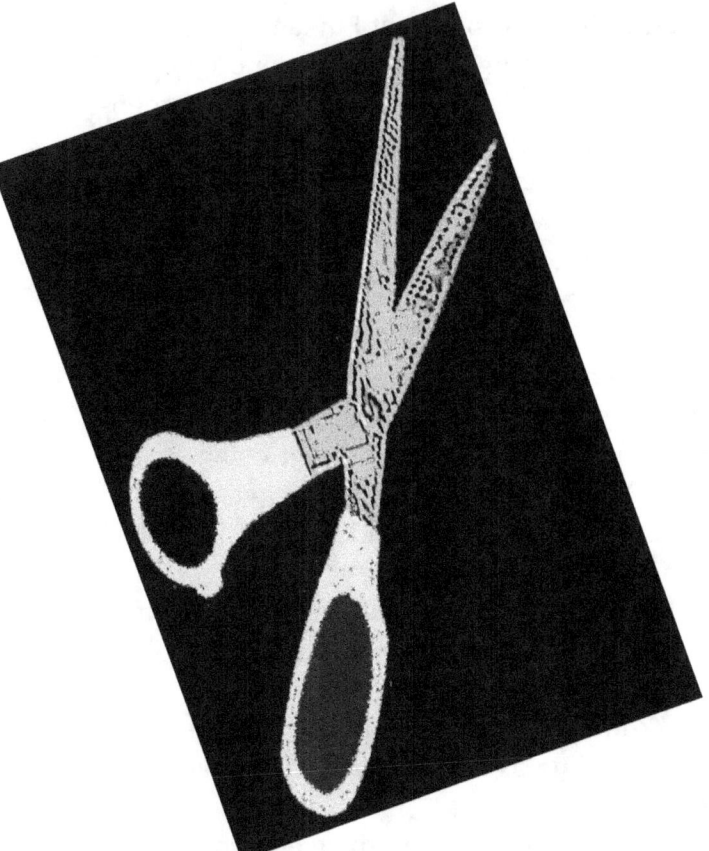

"Good Morning," I say to the Lunatic as I pass the reception desk, flashing my pearly whites. Easy, casual; like she isn't in the middle of a gooey-grilled-cheese-quality meltdown.

I know this expression well, that powdery sagging face of hers twists in a vulgar smile and those make-up caked lips pull back over her cheap set of horsey dentures. Really, the woman is old enough to live here rather than work here. There is some story behind that, how she never worked a day in her life until her successful hubby kicked the proverbial bucket and she found out the bucket was empty. Penniless and old enough to have grandkids in college (poor things) she was forced to take a job.

Not that I give a flying fart about what brought the beloved Lunatic to our office. She is here and I'm the one dealing with it, day after day. That's not to say it isn't entertaining. Hell, the retirement business isn't exactly full-of-

43

chuckles, if you know what I mean. At least she gives us something to break the monotony.

The Lunatic's bleached mass of nineteen-fifties sausage curls is already a frustrated mess at 8:57 AM. And to think, she probably suffered all night in wire rollers to achieve this now ruined look. Such a pity.

"Where are my scissors?" Her Press-On nails drum the desktop as our eyes meet briefly but her gaze darts, skitters away. The old gal is a twitching rat hot on the trail of some breadcrumbs and I can't help grinning at the image that blooms in my mind of her upturned nose sprouting whiskers and a stiff tail spiraling from beneath her knee-length skirt.

"What, you lost them again?" I offer, straightening out my features and controlling the grin. I glide past her into my office.

"You know he stole them," she hisses at Bess' backside as she followed me through the door.

"Don't you have something else you should be doing," Bess replies with a smirk I can hear in her voice. "Like some work? Possibly? You know, the reason you get the privilege of sitting at that desk and collecting a paycheck?"

Bess Brown, Ball Buster Extraordinaire. I should get her a plaque for her office with her new title. Maybe for Christmas.

"Yes," the Lunatic almost shouts, voice splintering. "I have plenty of work to do! But I need my scissors, *Adam*."

"I'll loan you mine," I call through my open doorway. "But I *will* need them back."

Oh, this is too much fun. I recommend every office have its very own psycho, seriously. If only every day could start with a smile, right?

A breathless groan comes from the room beyond but there's no time for this entertainment at the moment. The great yawning world of retirement living (or retirement dying, take your pick) awaits.

Don't get me wrong, I love my job-- or rather, I love success. Sure, I could have worked on Wall Street, could have spent my days sweating over mergers and stockholders and economic crashes. But why would I want to work myself sick to buy that late-model Beemer of my dreams, to have a view of the ocean from my penthouse condo? Who wants to work so hard? Not I.

No, this is my place, my life; a nice nine-to-five workweek, a fat paycheck, and only the slim possibility of developing migraines. But it has drawbacks, like any job.

My problem lies in the fact that I find it damned near impossible to look at a withered prune of a man, being fed strained peas by a careless nurse, and consider him a hero. Watching a watery-eyed woman struggling to describe a lecture she gave a million years ago, trying to retrieve dates and names that memory long since devoured, is even worse. Life is no longer a timeline of accomplishments but of successful bowel movements. The quality of their lives is measured by the quality of their daily visit to the toilet.

But the truly unfortunate part, besides just living in a world made of and ruled by crap, is the ability the residents retain to recall a time when life was something more. It's kind of terrifying. Like Night of the Living Dead without the cannibalism. Maybe I should get a nice position at an Alzheimer's home. Seems to me like there is some comfort in the idea of mindlessness, with the body in a state of living decay. A big idiot grin and a nice empty head? That's how I'd want it if someone had to hold my prick every time I took a piss. Maybe that's just me.

In my neat little office, I find a yellow Post-It stuck to my computer monitor. In an angry scrawl were the words: *I want them back*. Laughing softly, I peel it off and drop it into the empty wastebasket.

See, The Lunatic was at Bridge Creek nine years before I started on as a part time Office Clerk. She couldn't keep up with her paper work, so they were forced to hire extra help to pick up the slack. A few months from my degree, and graduating with honors, they were grateful to have me.

I was over-qualified, reliable, organized, and professional. The Lunatic, on the other hand, was completely whacked out of her mind and it didn't take long to figure that out.

I'd come directly from exams one day for some light work: typing memos and organizing the nightmare filing system. I needed the hours and, hey, there is never a shortage of work in this office. She was lounging at the reception desk, as always, with a paperback in one hand and a frilly bookmark in the other. She looked up when I came in, cotton-candy lips tightening into what is probably an attempt at a smile.

"Adam, you put together that report for Wheeler? Yesterday?"

"Sure did," I said, taking my seat at the outdated typewriter. Everything in a retirement community seems to be old for some reason or another. Ancient typewriter, antique Xerox, brads that look like they've gathered dust for fifty years.

"How many copies did you make of that?"

"Two," I answered. "One for Wheeler and one for the prospects."

"Two? Really?"

I nodded.

"That's odd," she sighed.

"Why?"

"Because there are five paper clips missing from my desk."

I laughed, "You know how many paper clips are in your desk?" But when I looked up, her smile wasn't oozing anything anymore. Her arms were stiff across her gravity-defying Eighteen-Hour bra. She peered over the black frames of horn-rimmed glasses and I knew this was the beginning of something. I just didn't know what or how bad it could get.

Three days later a letter came from Wheeler asking that I not "disturb her work space" claiming she was "sensitive."

So, what, I borrowed her highlighter pen? A few paper clips? Her friggin' stapler? Give me a break, right? I'd just steer clear of her, I figured. Simple solution to a ridiculous problem.

Seemed like a great plan until the following weekend when I came in to type up a death notice. Three quarters of the way through I typed 'feathered' when I meant 'fathered'. The supply cabinet was locked and company policy required I not be given my own set of keys until my interim period of three months passed. As if my taking the job was just an underhanded scheme to make off with a case of White Out or a hundred-thousand Post-It notepads.

So, I was three quarters of the way through the final letter that will ever be written in regards to a man's life and I had a date with a blonde with curves like a late-seventies Corvette. The Lunatic will never know, I decided. I put the White Out back where I found it when I finished.

The next morning, she came from the storage room, tape dispenser in hand and scowl firmly set, as I stripped out of my raincoat in front of her desk. "My White Out goes in the upper *left* corner of my desk," she snapped. "And I believe management already spoke to you about touching my things!"

I laughed. I laughed all the way to my desk. I laughed until my eyes watered and my cheeks started to spasm. Little did I know just how appropriate those tears were, and how many more there would be.

The first order of business this morning is an appointment with the Activities Director, Vanessa Cod. Who are we kidding? How much activity is there to direct with convalescents and invalids? Activities Director. Translation: The over-paid-under-worked-professional-smiler. Maybe she needs a plaque too.

I find myself sitting across from her, squinting in the glare of her Hollywood-quality grin. She yammers about a poetry reading and I pretend to listen with interest while eyeing the swell of her heavy chest under a sheer navy blouse, undone two buttons below "appropriate". Freckled cleavage, black satin bra, lace fringe, flaming red hair pulled back so tight you can see her hairline flinch every time she smiles.

Finally, I say, "Really, it sounds great. My concern is that with so many of them hearing impaired..." *How much would a megaphone set us back?* Thick red lips, wet smile, as she launches into her spiel. Tiny wrists, dainty ankles, all soft curves and blushing pale skin. Relaxed posture, easy laughter.

Vanessa Cod is unlike the women I generally date. Women who rush through power-lunches and power-workouts and quick power-fucks before taking their power-naps so they can dash off to power-meetings and pretend they're masters of the universe.

No, Vanessa will stay the whole weekend and we'll take our time. I won't call her about the poet. I'll send a note and not until Thursday. Let her start to worry. She'll think I forgot all about her little performance. Then, next Friday I'll bump into her in the parking lot on my way to my car. Spark some conversation, mention dinner plans, *"eating alone in a little Italian Restaurant downtown,"* and invite her along, like an afterthought. Casual supper. Laughter. Wine. Yeah.

I take one last look at the sway of her ripe-tomato hips as she leaves with a flirty wave.

"Do I have any messages?" I ask, passing through reception on my way to the bathroom. The Lunatic mumbles something about what I can do with my messages but I let it roll when I see at least ten messages in the stack. Great, another hour before I can get some takeout and a double espresso. Back to the cluttered desk to hold a phone to my ear until it goes numb along with my brain and my will to live.

Returning from the jon, there are two Post-Its on my computer screen. Layered, one on top of the other, the top reads: *Give back my scissors or else...* Peeling that one back, the second reads:

*...SNIP! Snip.*

I laugh uneasily, tossing them in the trash, taking off my wire-rimmed glasses to massage the bridge of my pinched-nose. The price of stylish nearsightedness.

"That's enough," I call through my open doorway. No reply. "Why don't you take an early day? It's obvious you're too keyed-up to do anything constructive around here."

"I have plenty to do, if you'll keep quiet, thank you." Her voice is wrought iron. I can almost hear the swollen vein in the middle of her forehead pulsing.

Only four months after hiring me, Wheeler interviewed me for the Assistant Executive Director position. "She *has* been here nine years and she's applied too, you know," Wheeler said with characteristic lack of interest. "Give me one good reason why I should give it to you."

"I can give you a whole list of reasons, Mr. Wheeler. But I'll keep it simple," I replied confidently, adjusting the aggressive red tie at my throat. "For starters, you don't really want an assistant who follows you around counting paper clips all day." Crooked smile. Slight lift to the brow.

Wheeler broke up. "You're right about that!" He slapped his knee, hound-dog jowls wobbling.

We settled into relaxed grins and Wheeler's fingers made a steeple to rest his chins upon. He considered, weighing things, chubby finger drumming his bulbous nose. There was nothing to weigh and we both knew it. This was all a formality, a dotting of the i's and crossing of the t's. I had the job. I had it before I even took the chair across from him that day.

"Alright, Adam," he said finally. "It's yours."

William Wheeler. The boss man. The head honcho. The big cheese. As Executive Assistant, I could start that short climb up his drab grey tie and into his executive's chair. He is the highest-paid executive in the retirement business and rumor had it the Board of Trustees felt he was taking the concept of "nonprofit" too literally. But they hadn't let him go yet. So when I saw the part-time clerk ad, things just started clicking into place.

There is a plan. There is always a plan.

After my promotion, things became more bizarre with the Lunatic. Every single day she threw me an arctic glare, accusing me of some stupid thing or another. First, she swore I erased appointments from her date book. I suggested she write her appointments in pen. Next, she insisted I stole the master copy of the Incident Report so she would have to make a new one 'from scratch', like she was baking bread or something. I recommended she keep better track of her files. She kept a novel in her upper left desk drawer, that's how little work the woman did, a dime store paperback with some Herculean man ripping the clothes off a breathless wench on the cover. She raved one day, behind the closed door of Wheeler's office, "He ripped the last page out of my novel! See! Just look at this!"

Wheeler mumbled something indistinct, translating to: *I don't really care.* She ranted. She raged. She actually cried over the last page of a Harlequin Romance. For weeks after, she insisted I sprayed some kind of bug repellent on the fabric of her chair. She went home early every day. "The chemicals" were giving her a migraine.

So, today we are back to the scissors. She accused me twice before of stealing her scissors, less blatantly, and it doesn't surprise me much that we're going for round three.

The day crawls. By lunchtime, my molded curls unravel into a frazzled halo and the tie at my throat loosens. There is the price of the new Xerox machine to haggle over, a plumbing disaster on the fourth floor, a surprise licensing inspection, and the payroll company screaming about a fax they didn't receive on Wednesday. As if all that isn't enough, there's the angry woman on the phone whose Pulitzer Prize winning Grams fell and broke a hip.

"--But Ma'am, your grandmother has been asked repeatedly to buzz a nurse if she needs to use the restroom. Especially in the middle of the night."

"What are you saying? That it's her *fault*? What? She *had it coming*?"

"Not at all. What I am saying is that Bridge Creek is not, in any way whatsoever, legally or morally responsible for this very unfortunate incident."

"You'll be hearing from our attorney," she barks.

"He'll tell you the same thing that I just told you. But you should call him. Whatever it takes to put your mind at ease."

Click. Bitch.

The post-lunch stack of messages is twice the size of the first.

I wander into Bess' office, trying to buy myself a little time. I'm not feeling it today, whatever "it" is. Bess sulks behind a stack of paperwork so tall that I can only see the top of her head from the doorway.

"Want to go out tonight? Get some beers or something," I suggest.

Okay. Don't even think it. I am *not* asking Bess Brown for a date. Besides having a chest as flat as my own, hair that screams "barber shop", and broken teeth, Bess isn't into guys.

"Sorry, Adam," she says without looking up. "Headed down south this afternoon. Big tournament, remember?"

"Rugby, right. I don't think your teeth need any more abuse though," I tease.

"You go for those beers though," she says, finally eying me. "You look like you could use a few. And a lap dance."

Now there were four Post-Its on my computer screen.

STOP TRYING TO MAKE ME NUTS!
JUST GIVE THEM BACK!
EVERYONE KNOWS YOU TOOK THEM!
*FREAK!*

And good humor vacates the premises.

I fume out of my office, cross the hall, and barge into Wheeler's office. I can feel the bitch's eyes on the back on my head as I pass. The big cheese is sprawled out on the sofa but flies to his feet as I slam the door behind me. His suit, sleeves two-inches too long and pants two inches too short, is rumpled. His eyes are red, moist, and baggy. Napping? *Really?* The muddled panic in his eye and the uncomfortable color climbing his neck gives me a faint tremor of satisfaction but it's nowhere near enough. Not today.

*Assistant Executive Director*. Translation: The-guy-busting-his-balls-while-the-bossman-sleeps-on-his-sofa. Maybe I need a plaque too.

"Send her home, Wheeler," I state baldly, zero preamble.

"Whassat?" He rubs his heavy lids, smoothing bushy brows and stifling a Saturday afternoon yawn.

I hand him the Post-Its.

"She's been sticking these damned notes on my computer screen all day. I have work to do," I spat. *Your work, you fat, lazy, son of a—* "A *lot* of work and I don't need this crap today."

"Just shut your door," he sighed. "It's not a big deal. She's always been a nut. She isn't changing anytime soon, son. Just don't take her bait, right?" That's that. She'll be at Bridge Creek till her bones turn to dust. On the bright side, that really could be any day now.

But I want, just for a split second, to choke the wheezing, drowsy life out of Wheeler with his lousy canary yellow tie.

"Adam, you're letting things get under your skin. It's been one hell of a week."

*As if you would know?* "It has," I reply flatly.

"Call up one of your girls. Who are you seeing now, hm?" I blink at his expression, smiling like some dirty-old-man wanting to get his rocks off but too limp for masturbation, before turning slowly on my heel. I left his office without another word.

"I'm going to the third floor," I inform to the Lunatic. "If it's an emergency, page the upstairs desk."

"Leisure time?" Tone dripping sarcasm like acrylic nails on a chalkboard.

"I don't owe you any explanations." Alright. Okay. So, I'm starting to lose my cool. "And don't you *ever* question me again. Wheeler's on his last leg, lady, and he's the only thing standing between you and the unemployment office." The elevator doors close between us just as her eyes fire and the smirk slides off her face.

I'm off to the third floor Skilled Nursing Unit and zombie-mothers crying out to children dead since World War Two, android-papas urinating on the floor for a laugh. Here lives true helplessness.

Ms. Wimble and I were an accident. Ordinarily, I have a strict policy about fraternizing with residents. She's blind and spends a great deal of time sobbing incoherently, bites the aides when they try to change her Depends or wipe spittle off her chin but she calms to the sound of my voice every time I come to her door.

*"Come and read to me, Adam."* Her voice makes a song out of words meant for me, in staggering contrast to her usual shrieking. We mostly read *Dante's Divine Comedy*. I never find anything very humorous or divine about it. In fact, it makes my head ache if I read too long. But the old woman loves it. She says that life is a Divine Comedy, not death. She laughs like mad. She is never civil to another human being, as far as the staff knows. Today I really need her singsong voice, her powdery hands reaching for mine, to put the cockiness back in my step.

It isn't affection that brings me back, week after week, though I like Ms. Wimble better than most. It's the respect, like a steroid pumping my ego's sprained muscles back into shape, I can't resist. Pasty-faced nurses eyeballing the four-figure suit, straight smile, the dimples accenting my sculpted expression with undisguised desire is a real poise augmentation on days like today. Women I wouldn't take to bed on my worst day saying, *'Handsome and sensitive? What a package!'* somehow turns the day into a conquest instead of a death sentence. Yeah.

I get off the elevator, adjusting to the sterile atmosphere of fluorescent lighting and piss-stained linoleum as I make my way quietly down the empty corridor. If the zombies hear you, they start wandering out of their rooms in bathrobes smelling of bowels and sweat.

310. 311. 312. A wobbly, high-pitched, living-dead-voice cries out, "Robert? Robert! It's Mama, Robert!"

With my wits still safely ensconced in my skull, I slip into room 312. A fresh stack of linens sits on the foot of a bare mattress. A thick nurse comes out of the bathroom carrying a black garbage bag, whistling to herself. She freezes when she sees me standing there, looking curious and high-strung.

"Oh God," she whispers, gazing down at her scuffed shoes.

"Where is Ms. Wimble?"

"Oh *God*. Adam, we left a message… Oh, Jesus."

The nightstand is clear of the framed photos that used to live there, the ones Ms. Wimble couldn't see. Her wooden cane with the painted handle is not propped next to her bed. Her rose-colored robe isn't hanging on the hook on the wall. In fact, there is just a hole where the hook used to be.

"When?"

"This morning. Early. She had a heart attack last night and died in the hospital. It was quick. She didn't suffer much." This poor nurse looks like she wants to hug me, like she thinks I might break down in tears right here in this empty room.

"Christ." I knead the thunder cracking in my temples.

"Services are Sunday, I think. St. Joseph's."

"Of course."

"I really am sorry, Adam," the nurse ventures. "Do you want to sit down a minute?"

"No, I can't stay. I have a death notice to prepare and it should have been done hours ago." More friggin' paperwork. There goes my weekend.

Red-faced, demeanor wrecked, I return to the damned Lunatic and my office.

"You look awful," she croons. "Maybe you should get out tonight and have some fun?" She smirks and I grind my teeth so hard I think they might break.

"You took a very urgent message this morning," I say, straining to manage my tone.

"Oh?"

"Yeah, only I never got the message. Ms. Wimble? Ring any bells?"

In her best Donna Reed impersonation she says, "Sure. Ms. Wimble. Evil old gal. Died this morning." She props her chin in the palms of both hands. "There. Now I've delivered the message."

I could jump the desk and strangle her, right here and now. I could rip every Loving Care curl right out of her aging skull. I could. But I swallow the urge, rage into my office, and slam the door so hard the paintings in reception rattle against the wall.

My monitor is now completely covered in yellow Post-Its. Each is marked with the scrawl of a truly desperate person, a person who can't even steady her own hand. *Please?! Where are the scissors?* On some there are large block letters, on others a tiny script. Some repeat the phrase again and again.

I have to deliberately shake the chill from my spine before removing them, one by one. She must have used a whole pad of Post-Its. I wonder if I could write her up for wasting office supplies. Maybe.

I phone the newspaper, the florist, Ms. Wimble's daughter in Hawaii, Saint Joseph's Mortuary, and play phone-tag with the attending physician at the hospital. Then there is the documentation. Most people would be shocked at how much paperwork is involved in eldercare. An incident report has to be filed for everything that happens. If a patient forgets the name of the president, a report must be filed. Someone slips and falls, hurt or not, a report is filed. Nose bleeds, bed wetting, temper tantrums, lack of appetite, increase in appetite, or a missed bowel movement are all report-worthy. There are also nurse's logs including notes on things we might not think are report-worthy, at every station. Data and backup-data and backup-backup-data. But when someone dies? Protection of one's backside is the name of the game. Documentation is the best weapon against a lawsuit is Elder Care 101.

I can't believe it when I finally looked up at the clock and discover it's seven P.M. The phones stopped ringing hours ago, I imagine, but I didn't miss them.

*Oh, hell. I'll just take the rest home with me,* I think, shrugging into my coat and stuffing the madness into my leather briefcase.

The overhead lights are turned in the reception area, leaving only the dim yellow glow of an antique lamp to light the room. All the other office doors are closed, everyone gone. Bess is probably already gearing up to kick some ass at the rugby tournament. Wheeler is probably watching Jeopardy in his bed at home, next to his wrinkled wife. The Lunatic is probably rolling her hair into those wire curlers, preparing for another day of psychosis.

I reach the door but, with my hand on the knob, I have the feeling something is off. I take another look around. Everything is clean and weekend-quiet. I almost turn away, almost make a clean getaway. Then I see what's nagging at the edges of my exhaustion.

The Lunatic's purse and car keys sit on her desk. In all the years she's worked at Bridge Creek, as far as I know, she never once stayed a minute passed five o'clock.

An unnatural tremor of uneasiness swiftly kicks me in the stomach. An annoying lump rises to the back of my throat. Fear pinches the backs of my knees as I consider the strange scrawl on all those Post-Its, replaying the insanity of this entire day. Her role seemed like a footnote until now. I find myself wondering, *Just how crazy is she?*

Striding over to the bathroom door, I evince a secure air to the empty room that couldn't care less, and rap the door firmly. "Everything alright in there?"

No shuffling of nylons. No creaking toilet seat. No soft sighs or mild groans. No rustling polyester falling back into place.

I knock again, harder. "Hey. Are you in there or not?"

Nothing. Great. Friggin' awesome.

Another unexpected image blossoms in my head but this one feels a million miles from this morning and doesn't make me snicker: The Lunatic crouched with a double-barrel shotgun perched on her padded shoulder, shrieking, *"Where are my scissors?!"*

Still, I push the door and peer in on the two gleaming stalls. One door stands open to an empty bowl while the other is closed with a pair of square-toed pumps visible beneath.

"I need to lock up," I say coolly, voice checked and posture erect.

Nothing.

*Okay,* I tell myself, *she asked for it.* I cross the short distance to the stall, pushing the door, unsurprised when it swings open. I've been on maintenance for weeks about fixing these old latches but they just never seem to get around to it. And how glad I am, at this moment, they didn't.

Laughter.

*Oh God…*

The kind of laughter that seems like it might kill you because your lungs seize and every muscle in your body spasms.

"Alright," I howl, "Alright! You win!" I collapse against the outer wall of the stall, hiding my face in my arm because I know if I look again, I'll never stop laughing. The sensation takes me over. My chin aches, my lips go numb, my ribs cry out, and still the laughter holds me tight, rebounding off the tiles and reverberating through this room that has suddenly become the most beautiful place in the whole entire world. Tears stream down my clenched cheeks. I don't know how much time passes, seems like hours

quake hilariously by, before I can look up again without dissolving completely.

There she sits, upon a sparkling porcelain throne, as dead as poor Ms. Wimble but without a fraction of the dignity. Her support hose are tangled around her varicose ankles, white granny panties rest just at the varicose shins, skirt gathered tightly in one varicose fist while her eyes, empty saucers, stare vacuously at me from an awkward angle. Her head rests against the stall, bricked-in dentures bared in a final grimace.

But it is the vein that brought on the hysterics, only now mellowing, the one running through the center of her forehead. It is just about as big around as a garden hose. But it isn't pulsating, as it so often has in the past on days like this one.

"Alright," I say, breathless. "You win, okay? I took your damned scissors! I did!"

From the inner pocket of my tweed blazer, I produce the red-handled scissors marked with a "Property of…" label.

"You still want them back?"

Silence. Guess she doesn't need them anymore.

I laugh my way back into the reception area and place the scissors neatly on her desk. I put her purse and keys back into the lower left hand drawer and chuckle earnestly all the way to my car, grinning helplessly. This grin will become painful soon but this light-headed end to a heavy-headed day is completely worth the ache.

As I pull into my driveway, I imagine maybe I'll run a little late Monday morning. Thinking better of it I decide to play it safe and call in sick. I just don't think I'll be able to keep a straight face any time before Tuesday.

◆————————————————————————◆

# Grace Notes Memory Books: The Most Memorable Gift You'll Ever Give

Grace Notes Memory Books are professionally printed and bound, designed as a collaboration between you and your GN specialist. Your custom memory book may include not only your favorite photos but your own memories, professionally written in entertaining, sentimental, and heartfelt prose styles to preserve those moments forever. A gift to last beyond a lifetime, to carry your story into the future, for generations to come, preserving for all time the history of you, your family, or that special occasion!

Memory Book Package includes professionally designed cover art/graphics, interior layout, and professional writing services (plus required research/interviews), photo touch-ups, as well as complete consultation. Books are manufactured on-demand so you can choose to print a few or a few dozen- even a few hundred- and pay only the cost of printing for each copy, as low as $3.00 each.

## Grace Notes Memory Books: Possibilities as Endless as Your Imagination!
## Preserve Your History or Commemorate a Special Occasion!

- Your Love Story & Picture Perfect Wedding: Tell your story in photos and antidotes for your children and their children!
- Document a Pregnancy & Birth of a Baby: You don't want to lose a single moment of the most important event of your lifetime! Preserve your photos and let our writers turn your memories into stories to be shared for years to come!

- Your Family History: Preserve Old Photos and Memories of Earlier Generations! Our writers will interview you and your family to create a rich book to withstand the years ahead and carry your history into the future!
- New Home or Business: Big moments should be treasured, your accomplishments treasured, and shared with those who cheer you on in your life!
- Anniversary: Mom and Dad or Grandma and Grandpa have a wonderful story of love, partnership, and triumph worth celebrating! Give the gift of that story.

Whatever your memory, we can help you turn it into a beautifully bound book to last the ages and to share with your loved ones!

## Find Out More @ www.GraceNotesBooks.com

# An Echo From the Stars

*Raymond Greiner*

Preparing for winter. It is mid-October and the color is spectacular. I anticipated a less colorful autumn since it has been so dry. It's the driest of the ten years I have lived here. The pond is very low; we desperately need rain. Early summer rains yielded these fall colors lessening the disparaging experience of drought.

The sun falls low earlier now. For a brief time, as the sun's trajectory lowers, it's blocked by the trees just west, but filters through open spaces and on the eastern side of the property the beautiful color of maple, oak and hickory leaves are highlighted like a spotlight shining on them. This is a short show, but it is a spectacle.

Daily we are bombarded by world news exposing a variety of events. Political posturing fabricating exaggerated promises and agendas seeking election. Globally there are incidents of heroism, medical breakthroughs and social unrest in a profusion of activity, humanity in motion.

I often think of this unfolding of things, wondering how it all fits into Universal design. There is such a mix; some aspects of human interaction are inspiring, creating cohesiveness, bonding and strengthening the human experience. Love of family, a sense of spiritual connection to nature, alignment with chosen religions, the desire to reproduce and create a better world for those of future generations, idealistic empowerments encouraging spiritual growth, and meaningful direction. The dark side of humankind is more difficult to understand or discover reason. The horrific evils that haunt our species are of no value to our development toward peaceful coexistence or spiritual enlightenment. These atrocities are beyond logic;

53

yet, continue, expanding and often dominant.

The Universe is a mysterious mass; knowledge and understanding emerge as the force of time marches to the cadence of Universal rhythms. The most significant reality is we would not exist without Universal pulsating expansion. The evolution of the Sun is what created life on Earth, about 1 billion years ago. The Earth is 4.5 billion years old, but until the Sun expanded to a certain size enabling life to form, Earth was barren. As I view the magnificence of autumn, I think of this. All life on Earth has been created from the evolution of the Sun. We are absolutely connected to the Sun, the Universe.

In a general sense our minds are incapable of fathoming the vastness of the Universe, it's beyond human comprehension, and because of this the tendency is to place it secondary in our thoughts. However, approaching it with imagination, combined with knowledge, enhances connective ability, creating personal Universal empowerment.

Humankind has been drawn to the stars since the earliest times. In this modern era many react to star thoughts in a mundane manner, disregarding cosmic significance, casting off Universal immensity, choosing the mentality: "Why bother with something that weaves its fabric with threads in billions when the human tapestry is so small by comparison?" The argument is that small by comparison does not cancel out importance. We are important, as important as any particle of matter within the entirety of the Universe; thus, should react to it from that scope of thought. The ancients were very connected to Universal power.

There have been mysterious events throughout Earth's history. Many remain locked in time, things that occurred long ago and often without written history, and as we observe physical evidence of these mysteries we fail to comprehend precise understanding of what they represent, tending to relate from a modern perspective, requiring tangibility. It may be that ancient cultures were less distracted than we of this modern era; faith and spirit occupied a penetrating force within their day-to-day design of living. The ancients were astute in their recognition of the power of natural functions, they were in awe and wonder, embracing Earth's ebb and flow, dancing with life, learning to blend and thrive in a world structured from a base of natural blessings, simplistic, earth-born activities, creating opportunity to visualize and extract Universal importance, establishing spiritual presence.

I was fortunate to attend a series of lectures by the futurist Barbara Marx Hubbard in Sarasota, Florida in the mid '90s. Her lectures highlighted humankind and its relationship to the Universe. Barbara's thinking is that humankind is presently in extreme infancy, extrapolating the time span of human existence to the age of the Universe, and the Earth. Science teaches that the Universe is in excess of 14 billion years old, and its life and ability to expand and grow is likely infinite. Science also reveals that humans, similar in stature to humans today, have been walking the planet for only 200,000 years. Barbara believes humankind will experience massive changes, suffer horrific events, but ultimately will expand and grow from these reversals and continue to develop as a species, attaining a zenith far more advanced than present day. If we have come this far in 200,000 years, imagine what we will be like in a billion years. As we know, change jumps to the quantum as it develops and moves forward. This is the crux of Barbara's message, that as we gain a closer time connection to the Universe, we will become more intensely connected to its overall force. In her view, we are very primitive, compared to what we may/can/will become. Things like hate, wars and inequities will not exist, as we become more profoundly developed spiritually, gaining an ability to reach higher within ourselves, releasing a broader level of compassion and understanding, and embracing the complexities of life with greater knowledge and inner love; achieving greater significance, meaning and purpose.

There is also much evidence that star connections have been exhibited on Earth in physical form, and as difficult as this is to grasp, bits of evidence are also difficult to ignore. In South America there are long strips of straight road-like lines, displaying symbolic ground images, shapes that are only recognizable from a high altitude located on mountaintops. There is a lake named in ancient times, "Rabbit Lake", but the shape of a rabbit is only visible at 3000 feet in altitude.

The Pyramids were largely ignored for over 3000 years, until the Greeks took a slight interest in them. Modern archeologists have been astounded by certain findings regarding the Pyramids. These are very large structures, and measurements from corner to corner are within 6-inch tolerances. No modern buildings nearly the sizes of the Pyramids come close to that tolerance ability. The Egyptians of that era had no pulley or wheel systems available to maneuver such large blocks of stone, which were quarried across the Nile and moved to the construction site, and their internal main shafts align perfectly with the star Sirius. It makes one wonder. Some historians theorize that the Pyramids were not originally constructed as tombs, but were ultimately used as tombs. The irony is from then on throughout Egyptian history, tombs were constructed in a more conventional manner in the Valley of the Kings, and no Pyramids were constructed beyond the time of the great Pyramid's construction era. The Pyramids, when they were new, were finished smooth, shined in sunlight, and had all-important capstones, which were eventually plundered and looted. There is no way of knowing the true history or purpose of the Pyramids.

One compelling detail has emerged in modern times. An ancient tribe of people, the Dogon, migrated to W. Africa from Egypt. Their origin is from the vicinity of the Pyramids during time of Pyramid construction. According to Dogon oral tradition, the star Sirius has a companion star, which is also depicted in ancient Dogon cave drawings. This star is invisible to the naked eye, but the Dogon had knowledge of this star and also knew that it orbits Sirius every 50 years. Two French anthropologists, Marcel Grianule and Germain Dieterlen, recorded it from a Dogon priest in 1930. This legend may be of little interest, but it is exactly true. How did a people who lacked any form of astronomical device know so much about an invisible star? They also knew that Jupiter had 4 major moons and that Sirius's small companion star was extremely dense, as science would later discover. One teaspoon of matter from this tiny star would weigh 5 tons on Earth. The star, which scientists eventually named Sirius B, was not officially seen or recorded until the late 19th century, when telescopes were developed enough to see this star. It was not photographed until 1970.

According to Dogon ancient oral history, a race of people from the Sirius system called the Nommas visited the Earth. They also appear in Babylonian, Acadian, and Sumerian myths. According to Dogon legend the Nommas lived on a planet that orbits another star in the Sirius system. They landed on the Earth in an ark that made a spinning decent to the ground with great noise and wind. It was the Nommas who gave the Dogon knowledge of Sirius B, and they may have been responsible for the Pyramid construction. The Sirius system is close in proximity to Earth, eight light years, and by comparison to the depth of the Universe a 20-minute commute. The furthest known distance in our Universe is 13 billion light years, a fascinating comparison.

What can these revelations possibly mean, or how can- or does- it affect people of our era? Much can be hypothesized, and compounded into various assessments. The ancients can serve as our guides: we are their reflection, as we may be to those who replace us in say 100,000 years. Looking at the ancients more closely, the Neanderthals represent a good starting point. Anthropologists tell us beings much like ourselves were first known of 200,000 years ago and called MHS (modern human species). Yet, earlier species appeared before MHS and among the earliest were the Neanderthal: their history goes back 500,000 years. They were a bit different, smaller, very stoutly built, had short life-spans, around 30 years however, they represented much more than that.

Modern views depict the Neanderthal as dull-witted, slow thinking, lacking in creativity, with low-level mental processes. Nothing could be further from the truth. The Neanderthal depicted the essence of the human spirit with great ability to transcend challenge and adversity. The Neanderthal's brain was larger than modern humans, but science tells us their brains functioned differently, they could calculate basic survival rudiments, create tools directly from the Earth, taught themselves how to hunt, gather food, manufacture clothing from animal skins, as they connected to the Earth more profoundly than any form of human beyond their time. They migrated from Africa to what is now Europe, and went as far north as what is now Russia. They taught themselves to endure extreme cold and survive in high, harsh latitudes, an amazing feat. I have spent blocks of time in wilderness areas using modern high-tech equipment, and the conditions are often challenging. To imagine starting from nothing, it is astonishing to think of how they were able to learn to function and thrive. Yet they did, exemplifying how diverse and flexible humans can be.

Neanderthals disappeared about 40,000 years ago, and many anthropologists surmise that the MHS eventually moved into the regions occupied by the Neanderthal, and a form of assimilation or destruction occurred resulting in their demise. This is theory. The specifics remain a mystery.

As we contemplate the immensity of the Universe, comparing it to our individual lives, we seem miniscule. However, visions we create within our minds and spirits reflecting the events of our lives are as golden as the Universe wholly. As we sluice the gravel from the creek we are given, representing our time on Earth, the nuggets we find are where we discover a love of life and a

recognition that we not only have purpose, we reflect the past and project the future. We are the Neanderthal, we are the modern, new, high-tech species; we are the gardeners that grow the wheat that feeds the next generation, which moves on and repeats the ever-present life energy.

In 1970, I lived in another place, also rural. My neighbor, Mr. Davis, lived across the road. He was in his 80's when I met him. I visited him at his house, where he was born, and lived with his sister his entire life. He invited me in, proudly showed me a photo album that dated back to the early years of the 20th century, with photos of him during the only time he did not live in this house, when he was a soldier in WWI. I was so enthralled.

We sat on his porch and had tea, and I mentioned to him how beautiful those big hardwoods that surrounded his house were. These were all mature trees. Mr. Davis told me he planted them all when he was a boy. I visualized a young boy planting the seedlings that were now majestic giants. This experience offered me a realization that we can and do leave a mark as we traverse life. He also told me of a tornado that came through the area in 1910, which knocked all the windows out of his house. The property where my house is located was a cabin and it was destroyed. My house was built in 1911 and Mr. Davis, in his youth, watched the carpenters work there each day.

A few of us will make it to the century mark. Most won't, but it's of less importance how long we live than what we do with the time given. It was late evening when I left Mr. Davis's porch, the moon was shining through his big oak tree. As I walked across the field to my house, stars filled the sky and I found Orion, it was a sensuous moment. I then squinted my eyes and looked skyward, seeing the stars in a diffused blur, and it seemed I could hear an echo.

◆——————————————————◆

# Mojave Green

*Jeffrey Miller*

All I wanted after pulling my sixth consecutive twelve-hour shift on the flightline was to crawl in bed and sleep for a week, but I couldn't. Instead, I lay in bed staring at the cracked, yellowed ceiling and wondering why my wife's first husband was coming to visit.

No sooner had I arrived home an hour earlier and gotten undressed than Betsy told me that Mitch was in town and wanted to see her.

The window fan rattled as it nudged the last of the cool night air across the room. Outside, the wind hissed through a Joshua Tree. In the distance, a peal of thunder rolled across the desert as a few F-16 fighters took off—probably some of the ones that I worked on last night.

I grabbed a crumpled pack of Marlboros on the nightstand and stuck one in my mouth. "When?"

"He didn't say." Betsy sat down on the edge of the bed. She brushed a wisp of blonde hair off her freckled forehead. "Sometime today."

She stared out a window that faced the desert toward the air base. Another F-16 took off, the roar of the engine as the afterburner kicked in rippled in the sky overhead Adelanto, the town we lived in near the base.

"He doesn't know we're married."

"I don't think you should be here when he stops by."

"Why didn't you tell him that you don't want to see him?"

"He says he wants to talk. It's the least I could do." She stood and moved over to the closet. "I don't have anything nice to wear."

She pulled out a powder-blue cotton print dress and held it up. I bought that dress for her in San Diego last month. She complained that it made her look too fat. She hung it back up and searched for something else to wear.

"You look fine."

"I don't want him to see me like this."

I stared at the tight yellow shorts and white halter-top she's wearing. The shorts rode high on her butt and wouldn't take anyone with half an imagination to know what was inside. Maybe I didn't want him to see her like this.

"Throw on a pair of jeans."

"They're all dirty." She rooted through pile of clothes at the side of the bed and threw some of the clothes onto the bed. Near the bottom, she pulled out a pair of faded jeans. "You're acting calm about this. When he finds out—"

I cut her off. "He's going to find out sooner or later. He's got at least one friend in the squadron."

"You don't know him. He's probably been drinking. He would never come back here unless he's been drinking."

I did know the way he got, especially the drinking, the gambling, and the fighting. Redlined for promotion three times; at least two Article 15s that I knew of. I knew him by name only—he had been assigned to a different section, but no one that I knew in the squadron ever spoke well of him. He was always in up to his ass with the Security Police, our CO, the First Sergeant, and the other crew chiefs.

Once, at the NCO Club, I walked in just after one of his escapades: he had started a fight with some crew chief that I worked with and it got ugly quick—broken chairs, a table, and a mirror behind the bar. I probably could have gotten in a few punches had I gotten there earlier. It had to be broken up by the Security Police, who ended up hauling five guys away.

Betsy didn't tell me much about him, except that they'd had some problems, and often, that she felt sorry for him. Six months after he was sent overseas, Betsy filed for a divorce. Three months later, we were dating.

The thought of him making a scene entered my mind. "Maybe I should hang around."

"No, that's okay. He won't try to pull any shit." She took off her halter-top and slipped on a bra. "Maybe you can drive into base or town."

"Just let me get a few hours of sleep." I stretched out on the bed and stared at the ceiling. There weren't this many cracks in the ceiling when we moved in a few months ago, but then that was before the new runway was built—before the fighters started to take-off and land over our apartment.

In next room, I heard Betsy singing a song made famous by the group Journey back in the seventies. I grabbed another pillow on the bed and scrunched it over my head to drown out the singing.

I hated Journey and she knew that.

I woke up sweating. I glanced at the clock on the dresser. Eleven o' clock. Three hours of sleep. What the hell was I going to do on base? Well, at least I didn't have to go into work tonight. After pulling six straight twelve-hour shifts I had the next two days off.

After I splashed some cold water on my face and brushed my teeth, I felt better. I finished a cigarette before I slipped into a pair of jeans and a T-shirt and walked out into the living room. Betsy worked a broom across the worn, faded black and white checked linoleum floor stirring up a cloud of dust as I shuffled toward the sofa. She opted for the jeans and the same halter-top-minus the bra. Lipstick, rouge, and blue eye shadow completed her ensemble. Just last week she complained that it was too hot to bother with makeup. I reached underneath the sofa and grabbed my sneakers. I glanced up at Betsy as she passed with the broom. Nail polish.

Betsy caught me staring at her. "I don't want him to think—"

I waved her off. I was in no mood to get into it with her now. "I'll be back in a few hours."

She intercepted me halfway toward the door. "You knew there was the chance this would happen."

I looked past Betsy to the screen door.

Betsy grabbed my arm. "I've dreaded this day, too."

She kissed me on the cheek, but tried not to smudge her lipstick.

I stopped before I reached the screen door. A rusted brown pickup truck came to a halt right in front of the door. As a cloud of dust settled around the truck, a tall and lean man climbed out. Standing up straight, he stretched and pushed his aviator sunglasses up his sunburned nose. He reaches down to straighten faded jeans over scuffed brown boots with thin arms covered with tattoos. He ran a hand through oiled hair and worked up a gob of mucous from his throat which he spat into the sand in front of him.

I backed away from the door just as Betsy saw the truck and Mitch. Mitch moved his head left to right as he walked to the front door.

Mitch rapped hard on the screen door and peered in through the door over his sunglasses. Betsy took a deep breath and exhaled slowly before she opened it. They stood in front of each other for a few awkward seconds before Mitch finally leaned in to attempt a hug. Betsy stood in front of Mitch with her arms at the side and allowed him to put his arms around her before she backed away a few steps.

Mitch removed his sunglasses and surveyed the apartment. "Place looks the same." He retrieved a toothpick from behind his left ear and stuck it into his mouth as he walked past Betsy.

"Mitch, this is—"

"I know." Mitch reeled around and stuck out his hand. "Can't keep secrets around here."

He rolled off a dry laugh that is part snort, part cackle.

I shook his hand, but withdrew quickly, as if I touched a dead fish. "I was on my way out."

"Nice to meet you, Dude." Mitch plopped down on the sofa and stretched out his legs over the coffee table. "Yessir, this place hasn't changed."

"I'll be okay," Betsy whispered.

Outside, as I walk toward our Toyota, I hear them laugh. I wonder if I shouldn't stay.

Even though I knew Betsy had been married to Mitch when we first started seeing each other, it wasn't until our wedding night in Vegas that she told me about the divorce. There we were, getting ready to consummate our marriage, as if it needed any consummating, when she told me all about the divorce. She told me how she took off for Tijuana with her best friend, who just went through a divorce there, and recommended the same attorney—some storefront divorce attorney named Rodriquez. It took thirty minutes and four hundred dollars. Betsy never did tell me why Mitch didn't contest.

"He's out of our lives now," Betsy assured me, as she snuggled up next to me in bed in our hotel next to the airport. "He'll never bother us."

Banging a guy's wife while he was on deployment was one thing, but stealing her away from the poor sucker was an entirely different set of circumstances. I felt a little uncomfortable at first when Betsy told me all these "details"—not that they would have made any difference but it would have been nice to know before we said "I do" at the Silver Bell Wedding Chapel. No matter what kind of assurances Betsy had for me, I knew it was only going to be a matter of time before Mitch came back wanting to get back what was rightfully his.

And when he did come back, I was going to have to be ready for him.

Instead of driving all the way into base I turned down Bartlett Avenue and drove a few blocks to the Hangar Inn. Back before I got married I used to come here with the other crew chiefs when our shift ended. Strictly a beer joint due to some stupid local ordinance, the place was famous for its homemade pizza. However, the real reason why it was so popular with the guys on swing shift was that it was the only place opened, and the owner, Barb Larson, would keep it open until morning.

When I pulled into the parking lot, there was only one other car at the far end. I recognized who it belonged to immediately. It wasn't Barb's car, though. It was Felicia Villanueva's banged up Chevy Impala. A couple guys in the squadron said she was bartending there now.

As I pulled up alongside of it, I noticed that it still had the cracked windshield from the time we went joyriding in the desert.

First Mitch and now Felicia—I couldn't wait to see what fate had in store for me next.

I walked in out of the bright sunshine into the darkened room and stood at the door waiting for my eyes to adjust to the darkness. The familiar strains of "Hotel California"

## Targetlove Pillow Talk

I feel such bliss
I say to myself
"I wish I could bottle this"
we're lucky we have each other
that we can be so close
spending hour after hour
yah know
I once dated a man that had
a penis the size of my index finger
No. I didn't laugh
and anyway it wouldn't have mattered
he was used to the way women reacted
having had so many in the sack
and he did just fine with it
But Oh! Guess what? He was married
well just a bit
the man with a little dick
turned out to be
one hell of a big prick
and the girls in the office
never warned me about him

*Richard Hansen*

emitted from a jukebox to my left.

"Hey stranger," a familiar voice said from behind the bar.

"Hi Felicia," I said, walking straight ahead to the bar.

She reached over and kissed me on the cheek.

"How's married life treating you?"

She had cut her hair and lost some weight since the last time I saw her right before Betsy and I got married.

"Don't ask."

"Poor baby, miss me already?" She laughed with a throaty, raspy laugh from years of smoking. Even though she had lived in the States for over ten years, she kept her accent. "What can I get for you?"

"Beer," I said, smiling.

"Mitch is in town," she said, pouring me a glass of Oly from the tap. "He was in here last night, asking about you."

"News travels fast," I said, taking a sip of my beer.

"Hey babe, this is Adelanto. You know you can't keep no secrets here."

"I know. He's at the apartment now."

"He's where?"

"At the apartment."

"What does he want?"

"He didn't say."

The door opened and two men entered. They looked toward Felicia and me before they walked to the far end of the bar. I watched her sashay down the length of bar and wait on the two men. She still filled out a pair of tight jeans better than women half her age. She had a few miles on her now, but she looked just as good and hot as she did the night I met her at the Airman's Club my first week at George a little over a year ago.

"Be careful. There's no telling what he'll do."

"I can take care of him," I said finishing my beer.

"If things ever go south, just in case, you still got my number, right?"

When I arrived back at the apartment two hours later, his truck was still in the driveway. I saw Betsy peering out the living room window as I near the front door of the apartment. Calling the shack we lived in an apartment is an understatement. Back during World War II, the Army Air Corps bought out all these chicken ranches with their long buildings and converted them into temporary barracks. Supposedly they were supposed to have been torn down after the war, but they were converted into low-rent apartments. Nearly fifty years later, these same buildings, with some improvements over the years, were still standing. Now some slum landlord rented them out to guys like me, who couldn't get base housing.

Before I reached the door, Mitch and Betsy walked out. Mitch had an arm around Betsy's shoulder.

"Mitch wants to talk to you. I'm going into town to see Kimberly." Betsy walks past me toward the Toyota. "There's some pizza in the icebox."

Mitch laughed.

I started to move back to the car, but Betsy's already started it up and put it in gear.

"Don't wait up for me if you're tired." She checked her makeup in the rearview mirror.

Betsy backed the car up, and spun the tires in the sand before she tore out onto the blacktop road. We both watched the car move down the road until we can't see it anymore.

"You're one lucky dude. Can't say that I envy you, though. I had my chance," he rocked back on his heels, gazing up into the sky. "Sweetest piece of ass I ever had."

"Excuse me?"

Mitch moved past me, kicking up some sand as he moves toward his truck. From the back, he pulls out a cooler. "Didn't want Betsy to know I had this. She used to get really bent out of shape with my drinking. I don't think I could have gone another minute without a cool one. Beer?"

"Listen, Mitch, if it's about—"

"You know why I'm here." He pulled out a dripping bottle of Budweiser, opened it on the lip of the truck's rust-flecked bumper and hoisted it to his lips. Beer streamed out the corner of his mouth that he wiped away with the back of his hand. "It's a hot one today. I don't know how you two can still live in this place. I figured you for base housing, being an E-5 and all. Betsy probably told you that I was redlined for promotion a couple of times because of my drinking. No promotion. No base housing. That sucked."

Mitch emptied the bottle. He pulls out another. I moved out of the sun to a picnic table shaded by one of the few trees we have on our lot. Mitch followed, dragging the cooler across the sand and wisps of brown grass.

"You sure you don't want a beer? I figured you for a beer man."

I nodded as I leaned back against the table. Mitch opened the bottle with the edge of his belt buckle and handed it to me.

"I'm not here to cause trouble. That's what I told Betsy. I'm not about to pull any shit. Those days are gone. What's done is done." He took a long drink and wiped his mouth again. "I'm not going to fuck with you, if you know what I mean."

"That's good to know."

"Uh-huh," Mitch grunted as he stuck a cigarette in his mouth. "What's done is done, as my old man used to say. You can't go back and unscrew the pooch."

As much as I despised hanging out with Betsy's ex, I had to hand it to him, he was a colorful character. Who knows, if things had been different, we might have been the best of buds. An F-16 screamed overhead. Mitch shaded his eyes with one hand as he looked up at the fighter streaking toward the base.
"What do you want to talk about, Mitch?"
Mitch followed the fighter as it circled over the base before it began its final approach.

"What do you want to talk about, Mitch?"

Mitch followed the fighter as it circled over the base before it begins its final approach.

"Yeah, I'm glad I don't have to fuck with them anymore." He turned toward me. "I only want what's mine."

*Here it comes.*

He chugged the rest of the beer and tossed the bottle into the desert. It hit a rock and shattered into brown shards. He grabbed another dripping one from the cooler. He wiped off the water with one quick move and popped it open.

"What?"

"Come on, do I have to spell out everything for you, Sarge? You and I both know it was wrong."

"Mitch, I don't know what you're talking about."

"Five thousand dollars. Does that refresh your memory?" Mitch stared at me with hooded eyes.

"What five thousand dollars?"

"You know god damn *what* five thousand dollars."

Mitch took another drink. The veins on his neck tightened. "I was sending Betsy most of my paycheck every month to put in our savings account. Turns out, while I was sweating off my ass in Saudi, she's sweet-talking some grease ball attorney in Tijuana and all the while cashing the checks. Like I said, I only want what's mine."

"Mitch, I really don't know what to tell you. Betsy never told me about any money. It seems that this is something you and Betsy have to work out."

Mitch leaned back and laughed. "Something Betsy and I have to work out? Yeah, ain't that a fucking joke."

"Wasn't that why you came back here? Doesn't she know?"

"What do you mean, she doesn't know? Of course she goddamn knows! She spent the goddamn money." He drank some of his beer and pointed a bony finger at me. "From what I hear, you two were screwing around when I was still sending her the money."

"Honestly Mitch, I didn't know anything about the money."

Mitch shook his head. "The way I see it, pal, you're just as responsible. Now, you don't want me to cause any trouble for you. E-5 and all. Might not look so good the next time you come up for promotion. And don't think for a moment I don't know about you and Felicia."

You had to bring her up, didn't you Mitch? If he wanted to threaten me by bringing in Felicia he was not as stupid as I thought. He knew that it would be hard to collect the money without a little leverage.

Mitch and I sat quietly for a few minutes watching dust devils spin across the baked ground. Mitch took a drag off his cigarette and let the smoke curl into his nose. He turned around on the picnic table and craned his neck toward the back of the apartment.

"I see Betsy got rid of my snake cages."

I shrugged my shoulders.

Mitch moved toward the back of the apartment, shaded by an emaciated tree. He surveyed the area and kicks a rock into the spot supposedly where his cages must have once stood.

"I used to hunt for snakes. It drove Betsy up the fucking wall. I had over fifteen cages and twenty snakes." He stretched out his arms to show where he had placed the cages. "You wouldn't believe how many people are misinformed about snakes. Did you know that a person is nine times more likely to die from being struck by lightning than by dying from a venomous snake bite?"

"No, I didn't know that."

"It's true. Out of the approximately 45,000 reported snake bites each year in America only 8,000 of those are venomous, but only around twelve people die from them," Mitch said, lowering his arms. "Have you ever seen a Mojave Green?"

"No, but I was warned about them when I arrived here."

"Let me guess, some dickhead butterbar told you about them during orientation?"

I nod.

"You're damn right you watch out for the Mojave Green! Meanest fucking snake I've ever come across." Mitch moved back to the table and swigged more of his beer; he rested one foot on the bench with one arm resting on his knee.

"The Mojave Green is a strange one. It's not like other rattlers. It packs a badass poison that goes right for the nervous system. That shit will fuck you up quick. I've only seen one in all my years of hunting for snakes. Sometimes it's hard to tell the difference between a Mojave Green and a Diamondback but I found out once.

"I was walking in the desert one morning, not paying attention to where I was going; you know, just walking. Well, I tripped over a rock and fell down. Dumb fucking luck, I thought when I started to pick myself up because at first, when I saw it moving—it was no more than two or three feet long—I thought it was a Diamondback. I've caught a few Diamondbacks in the past and you'd think I'd know my fucking snakes. But this snake had moved into the shadow of a Joshua Tree and I couldn't tell, at least not yet.

"After I got up, I tossed a rock at it to move it back into the light. Didn't budge. So I tossed another rock at it. I know what you're thinking, I should have gotten the hell out of there, but it wasn't like I was scared or anything. The snake coiled. The color froze me. I stood in my tracks."

Mitch took a drink and leaned forward. "The Mojave Green is a nervous one." He shot out two fang-like fingers toward my face just inches from my nose. "A real quick striker!"

He jerked back his fingers and leaned back. "That fucker just sat there all coiled up and ready for some action, but I was already gone. *Hasta la* fucking bye-bye. You want another beer?"

"No."

Mitch tossed down his beer. He picked up the cooler and moved back to the truck. After he set the cooler in the truck, he slipped on his sunglasses and climbed in. "I'll be in touch, dude."

I was in the apartment before Mitch backed out onto the road.

After I ate two slabs of the cold, rubbery pizza and washed them down with a can of pop, I walked out to a small metal storage shed behind our apartment. I had to move around a lot of boxes, mostly Betsy's crap until I come to my footlocker in the back. I opened it and took out a small wooden box, the size of a shoebox from inside.

Back in the apartment, it was still too hot to sleep, so I took a shower. I ended up on the sofa with a towel around me, watching TV. The phone rang twice, but each time I didn't get up to answer it.

Around ten, the apartment finally cooled. I moved into the bedroom, slipped on a pair of shorts, and stretched out on the bed. A breeze blew in from the desert.

A half an hour later, Betsy pulled up.

I heard her walk into the bedroom. I felt the mattress give as she reached across the bed to see if I was awake.

"It's about the money, isn't it?" Her voice was sharp and abrupt. She thumped me on the shoulders with the palm of her hand. "It's the money, right?"

I smelled whiskey on her breath and the same cheap cologne Mitch was wearing.

She nudged me again, but I still didn't answer. However, when she started to move off the bed, I jerked my body around and grabbed her wrist. "It *is* the money."

I released my grip. She backed away and stumbled over the pile of clothes at the side of the bed. After I heard the door click shut and the TV turned on, I got up and sat on the edge of the bed. I grabbed a cigarette from a crumpled pack of Marlboros, and lit up. I took a deep drag off the cigarette and looked out the window. It was a full-moon night and I could

see all the way to the base. You'd be surprised what you could see on a clear night like tonight.

After I finished the cigarette, I reached under the bed and slid out the small wooden box from my footlocker. I opened it slowly, and took out my pistol. The polished nickel-plated barrel caught the moonlight as I held it in my hand. It felt cool, comforting, reassuring against my skin. I watched the vaporous whorls of my fingertips evaporate quickly.

Yeah Betsy, I had secrets too.

I gently ran my hand across the barrel. I hoped the inside was not dirty.

◆――――――――――――――――◆

Jeffrey Miller has spent the last two decades flitting around Asia as a university lecturer and writer, including a six-year stint as a feature writer for The Korea Times, South Korea's oldest English-language newspaper. Originally from LaSalle, Illinois, he relocated to South Korea in 1990 where he nurtured a love for spicy Korean food, Buddhist temples, and East Asian History. He divides his time between South Korea and Laos, where his wife Aon, and three sons Bia, Jeremy Aaron, and Joseph reside.

He's the author of four books including War Remains, a Korean War Novel. The award-winning book won two Military Writers Society of America 2011 Book Awards: Gold for Literary Fiction and Silver in the Korean War category and was a finalist in the 2012 Global Ebook Awards.

Currently a history and English lecturer at the SolBridge International School of Business in Daejeon, South Korea he recently appeared in a Korean War documentary about the ongoing search for war remains in South Korea and one of the Korean War battles described in his novel War Remains. A previous incarnation of story originally appeared as part of Jeffrey's master's thesis in 1989.

Visit GraceNotesBooks.com for more info on this issue's contributors, subscription information, or to read excerpts from our book publications. The Grace Notes Foundation also hosts programs to support writers and other creative and we, as a non-profit organization, feel no shame at all in begging your support. Be it a cash donation, the purchase of a book title, a subscription to Notes, or picking up something from our original merchandising line—all revenue supports our many efforts to save the world from mediocrity.

www.ingramcontent.com/pod-product-compliance
Lightning Source LLC
Chambersburg PA
CBHW080544180626
46818CB00008B/3123